Long Island Wine Country

Long Island Wine Country

*Award-Winning Vineyards
of the North Fork and the Hamptons*

JANE TAYLOR STARWOOD

PHOTOGRAPHS BY BRUCE CURTIS

FOREWORD BY LOUISA THOMAS HARGRAVE

ThreeForks®

GUILFORD, CONNECTICUT
HELENA, MONTANA
AN IMPRINT OF THE GLOBE PEQUOT PRESS

To buy books in quantity for corporate use
or incentives, call **(800) 962–0973**
or e-mail **premiums@GlobePequot.com.**

Text copyright © 2009 by Jane Taylor Starwood
Photographs copyright © 2009 Bruce Curtis (except as listed below)

ALL RIGHTS RESERVED. No part of this book may be reproduced or transmitted in any form by any means, electronic
or mechanical, including photocopying and recording, or by any information storage and retrieval system, except as may be
expressly permitted in writing from the publisher. Requests for permission should be addressed to The Globe Pequot Press,
Attn: Rights and Permissions Department, P.O. Box 480, Guilford, CT 06437.

ThreeForks is a registered trademark of Morris Book Publishing, LLC

Long Island Wine Country is a registered trademark of the Long Island Wine Council. Used by permission.

Photographs on pp. vi, 1, 2, 3, 4, 13, 14, 16, 18, 36, 37, 38, 39, 40, 43, 44, 46, 49, 50, 51, 53, 57, 58, 60, 66 (right), 73, 75,
79, 80, 81, 82, 83, 84, 87, 91, 93, 98, 102, 105, 107, 108, 119, 122, 124, 125, 137, 138, 139, 140 (bottom), 143, 150-51,
152, 157, 159, 161, 164, 165, 167, 169, 171, 180 by Jane Starwood; pp. 20, 27, 28, 29, 30, 31, 70, 94, 103, 104, 129, 133,
134, 135 by Jane Starwood, courtesy of L.I. Wine Press, reprinted with permission of Times/Review Newspapers Corp.,
Mattituck, N.Y.; pp. 24, 25 courtesy Theresa Dilworth; pp. 55, 59, 61, 63, 127, 146, 162, 166, 168 by David Starwood

Background vine illustration throughout © Shutterstock

Text design by Sheryl P. Kober, Layout by Melissa Evarts

Library of Congress Cataloging-in-Publication Data

Starwood, Jane Taylor.
  Long Island wine country : award-winning vineyards of the North Fork and the Hamptons / Jane Taylor
Starwood ; photography by Bruce Curtis.
    p. cm.
  Includes index.
  ISBN 978-0-7627-4839-6
  1. Wine and wine making—New York (State)—Long Island—Guidebooks. 2. Vineyards—New York (State)—Long Island—
Guidebooks. 3. Long Island (N.Y.)—Guidebooks. I. Title.
  TP557.S725 2009
  641.2'20974721--dc22
                                                                                                    2008045825

Printed in China
10 9 8 7 6 5 4 3 2 1

CONTENTS

RECIPES

LONG ISLAND WINE COUNTRY

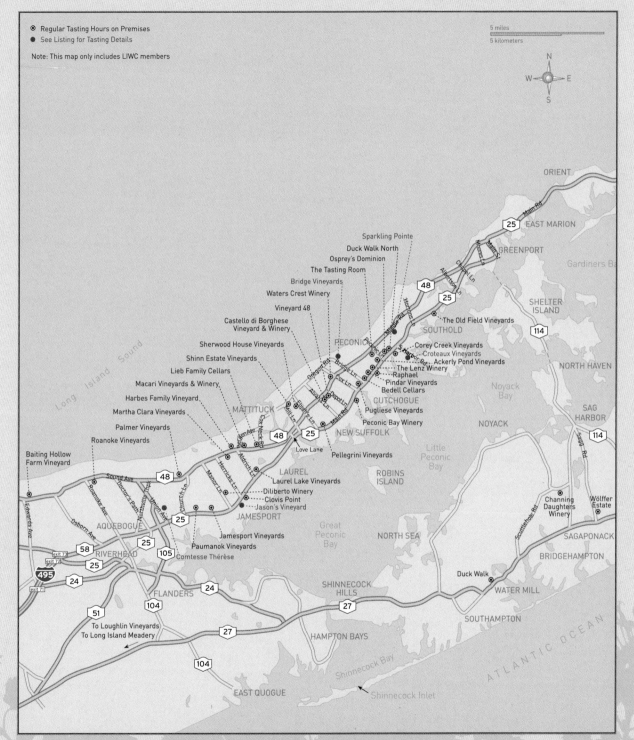

⊙ Regular Tasting Hours on Premises
● See Listing for Tasting Details

Note: This map only includes LIWC members

5 miles
5 kilometers

ORIENT

EAST MARION

GREENPORT

Gardiners Bay

SHELTER ISLAND

Sparkling Pointe
Duck Walk North
Osprey's Dominion
The Tasting Room
Bridge Vineyards
Waters Crest Winery
Vineyard 48
Castello di Borghese Vineyard & Winery
Sherwood House Vineyards
Shinn Estate Vineyards
Lieb Family Cellars
Macari Vineyards & Winery
Harbes Family Vineyard
Martha Clara Vineyards
Palmer Vineyards
Roanoke Vineyards
Baiting Hollow Farm Vineyard

SOUTHOLD

The Old Field Vineyards
Corey Creek Vineyards
Croteaux Vineyards
Ackerly Pond Vineyards
The Lenz Winery
Raphael
Pindar Vineyards
Bedell Cellars

PECONIC

CUTCHOGUE

Pugliese Vineyards
Peconic Bay Winery

NEW SUFFOLK

NORTH HAVEN

SAG HARBOR

Noyack Bay

NOYACK

Little Peconic Bay

ROBINS ISLAND

Long Island Sound

MATTITUCK

Love Lane

Pellegrini Vineyards

LAUREL

Laurel Lake Vineyards
Diliberto Winery
Clovis Point
Jason's Vineyard

JAMESPORT

Jamesport Vineyards
Paumanok Vineyards
Comtesse Thérèse

AQUEBOGUE

RIVERHEAD

FLANDERS

To Loughlin Vineyards
To Long Island Meadery

Great Peconic Bay

NORTH SEA

Channing Daughters Winery

Wölffer Estate

SAGAPONACK

BRIDGEHAMPTON

Duck Walk

WATER MILL

SOUTHAMPTON

SHINNECOCK HILLS

HAMPTON BAYS

Shinnecock Bay

Shinnecock Inlet

EAST QUOGUE

ATLANTIC OCEAN

Map courtesy the Long Island Wine Council, 2008

Whey Jane Starwood asked me to write an introduction to her book about Long Island wine, I was pleased, and also a little worried. I knew her skill as a playwright and as an editor, but how could she capture the essence of this small wine region, located ninety miles east of Manhattan on two narrow forks of sandy, sunlit land? When she sent me her first few chapters, I knew that she understood what winemaking is really about. Given the conditions that will allow the noble grape to grow, it is the individual winemakers, asserting a personal vision, a yearning desire, on the land and its fruits, who determine the style and reputation of a wine region. Jane chose to use the winemakers' own voices to tell their stories. Through their words their intentions, their hesitations, and their courage are revealed, hinting at the nature of their wines.

As the first vintner on Long Island's East End, I arrived on the North Fork in 1973, a twenty-four-year-old wine fancier with no agricultural experience at all. I had no voice to express my desire to take on the old potato farm I purchased with my husband, Alex, a scholar of Chinese politics and poetry who had no more farming experience than I. There were no contemporary voices of viticultural experts on Long Island, so we relied on far more ancient voices. Alex studied Roman poets of the first century A.D. Columella advised him to "admire a large estate, but plant a small one." So we began with a sixty-six-acre farm in Cutchogue, with a tiny farmhouse dating back to 1680. That it was a mouse-infested mess, with holes punched through its walls and a pistol dated 1884 buried under its attic walls, did not detract from its allure for us, in our desire to make a family and create our own sheltered existence.

From Dryden's translation (1697) of Virgil's *Georgics* (29 B.C.), we read the words that echoed our desire for "Easy quiet, a secure retreat / A harmless life that knows not how to cheat."

Another voice that touched our desire to grow grapes in a place where centuries of growing other, more hardy crops had essentially predicted failure for a plant as tender as the *Vitis vinifera* we dared to grow—starting with Pinot Noir, Cabernet Sauvignon, Merlot, Sauvignon Blanc, Chardonnay, and Riesling—was that of John Wickham. Wickham was the man we came to see on the North Fork in November 1972, after hearing of his success with similarly sensitive table grapes. Wickham—who also dared to grow other crops that allegedly couldn't be grown on Long Island—showed us his vines, still green at Thanksgiving time. He drove us to see Long Island Sound and Peconic Bay, three miles apart and crucial to the moderating influence of water on this microclimate. Then he said, "Don't be pioneers like me. Pioneers always pay twice."

With a challenge like that, who could resist? We immediately began looking for a farm to call our own. Once we found one, another voice, that of our farming neighbor, Mike Kaloski, informed our experience. Mike grew potatoes, but he loved seeing anything new. He showed us how to hitch up a tractor, run a cultivator, fix a pump. More importantly, after finding us still in bed at nine o'clock one morning, he told us: "You will never be farmers unless you begin work at six, eat lunch at noon, quit at six, and take Sundays off. What do you think the firehouse horn is for?"

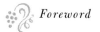

That made all the difference.

When it came to growing grapes and making wine, I wanted to listen to other voices. I wanted experts to tell us what to do. But there were no experts on Long Island. The first winter we pruned our vines, the leading expert from California visited at the same time as the leading expert from upstate New York. Looking at the same vine, one told us, "Choose the largest wood but cut off all lateral shoots." The other told us, "Keep narrow shoots and, if there are laterals, keep them."

After that I knew I had to find my own techniques that would work on Long Island, regardless of what might succeed in other regions.

By 1979 a few others had come to plant wine grapes on Long Island. The number of vineyards grew in fits and starts through the 1980s and 1990s. Some who came eventually abandoned their efforts and went back to writing jingles, making art, selling fashion, or whatever they had done before coming to eastern Long Island. Others stayed and, like myself, raised families as well as grapes.

In every case we were motivated by our voices. Few of us had previously farmed, or made wine. Some, drawn to winemaking for its creativity, couldn't bear the responsibility of running a business. Others never had the capital required to make it work. In my own case, after twenty-seven years of making dynamic, delicious wines, my husband and I split up, selling our farm to an Italian prince. My husband followed his intellectual muse, working the estate of his mind. I also went on in a literary way, writing a memoir of life amidst the vines, called *The Vineyard*.

The small farming towns of the North Fork are now suburbanized, but the broad, austere farms that remain keep inspiring new vintners, each with a personal voice, an individual desire to discover life through growing and making wine. The words of Virgil still resound:

Come strip with me, my God, come drench all o're
Thy limbs in must of wine, and drink at ev'ry pore.

—Louisa Thomas Hargrave

Arrival

It's your first trip to eastern Long Island. If you're approaching from the west, depending on the traffic, you've just crept or cruised past leagues of suburban sprawl on the Long Island Expressway. Soon you're passing through the Pine Barrens, where the highway is a wide gray ribbon strung taut between banks thick with evergreens. At last you see the sign heralding your imminent arrival in Riverhead.

In the heart of Riverhead's historic downtown, the Peconic River empties into the Great Peconic Bay, cleaving this long, narrow island jutting northeastward into the Atlantic Ocean into two narrow peninsulas. The North Fork stretches from Riverhead to Orient Point; the South Fork, known to the wider world as the Hamptons, ends at Montauk. Between the two forks lies Shelter Island.

As you approach the end of the expressway, the penultimate exit slices to the south, toward downtown Riverhead and the Hamptons, or hooks to the north, toward Sound Avenue and the Route 48 wine trail. But if you've decided to start your tour on Route 25, saving the northern trail and the Hamptons for later, you stay on the LIE until the very end, curving past Tanger Outlet Center, with its vast American flag, onto Route 58, also known as Old Country Road. Much to your dismay, the road mocks its bucolic name, herding you through the kind of clogged commercial corridor you thought you'd left behind.

And then, as you cross County Road 105, the landscape is transformed. You're now on Route 25, known to locals as the Main Road. You pass farmhouses set back on green lawns shaded by towering oak and maple trees, their massive trunks telling of ages gone by. Your white-knuckled grip on the steering wheel loosens and the tension in your shoulders starts to melt as you realize you've finally traveled beyond the land of megamalls, giant chain stores, and endless car lots.

Soon you catch your first glimpse of a vineyard basking in the sun, its broad leaves silently turning sunlight into sugar, ripening *Vitis vinifera,* the European grapes that make the world's finest wines. For a moment you might imagine you've been mysteriously wafted to the French countryside, but no, this is the East End of Long Island, the most exciting new wine region in North America. You've reached your destination, but your journey of discovery has barely begun.

Whether you come from east, west, north, or south, by car, ferry, train, or bus, Long Island's wine country will surprise and delight you with the beauty of its landscapes and seashores, its old-fashioned Main Streets and steepled white churches, the bounty of its fields and waters, the warmth of its people, and the quality of its wines.

In these pages, tucked among the vineyards, you'll find recipes from local chefs using local ingredients, with suggestions for pairing with Long Island wines, along with many photographs showcasing the beauty and bounty of the East End.

About This Book

The vineyards are presented by town or hamlet, from west to east. On the North Fork the book hops back and forth between the Main Road/Route 25 and Sound Avenue/Route 48 wine trails, but you might want to pick one of these trails and visit wineries along and near it, then come back by the

other trail, stopping in at the wineries there. Or you could pick a hamlet and visit the vineyards nearby. The North Fork is a small area, allowing you to be either methodical or haphazard and still easily take in as many wineries as you can handle during your stay.

The three wineries in the Hamptons are farther apart, but still within a short drive of one other. If you're planning to visit both the North Fork and the Hamptons in one trip, allow plenty of travel time, especially during the busy summer and fall seasons. You can either take the North Ferry from Greenport, drive across Shelter Island on Route 114, and take the South Ferry to Sag Harbor, or make the loop through Riverhead via routes 105 and 24. The map in this book will show you the way.

Unless you're here for a week or more, you won't be able to visit all the wineries in one trip. Peruse the book and plan your journey according to whatever criteria you choose: geography, your favorite kind of wine, the visual appeal of the tasting room, or a glowing recommendation from friends. Most of the wineries are open year-round, but days and hours of operation can vary with the seasons. If you're planning to visit a particular winery, especially during the winter, check the Web site or call before making the trip.

Each East End winery has its own special style that's evident from the moment you pull up to the entrance. That unique style is carried throughout, from the passion and dedication of owners and staff to the architecture of the buildings, the atmosphere in the tasting room, and the myriad decisions made by the winemaker and vineyard manager every step of the way from vine to wine.

By the time you hold this book in your hands, no doubt there will have been a few changes. New wines will be in release, and specific vintages mentioned here may no longer be available. New wineries and tasting rooms may have opened or established ones changed hands, and more small producers almost certainly will have appeared. These dynamics are part of what makes our wine region so exciting: It is ever evolving toward higher and higher quality, higher and higher status in the world of wine.

As you tour the wineries and taste their wines, you may be tempted to choose a favorite. That's all right, but don't let it stop you from exploring all of them as you return many times to the beautiful, bountiful East End. Remember, those who never venture into the unknown never find the hidden treasure waiting to be discovered at the next pour, in the tasting room just down the road.

—Jane Taylor Starwood

THE NORTH FORK

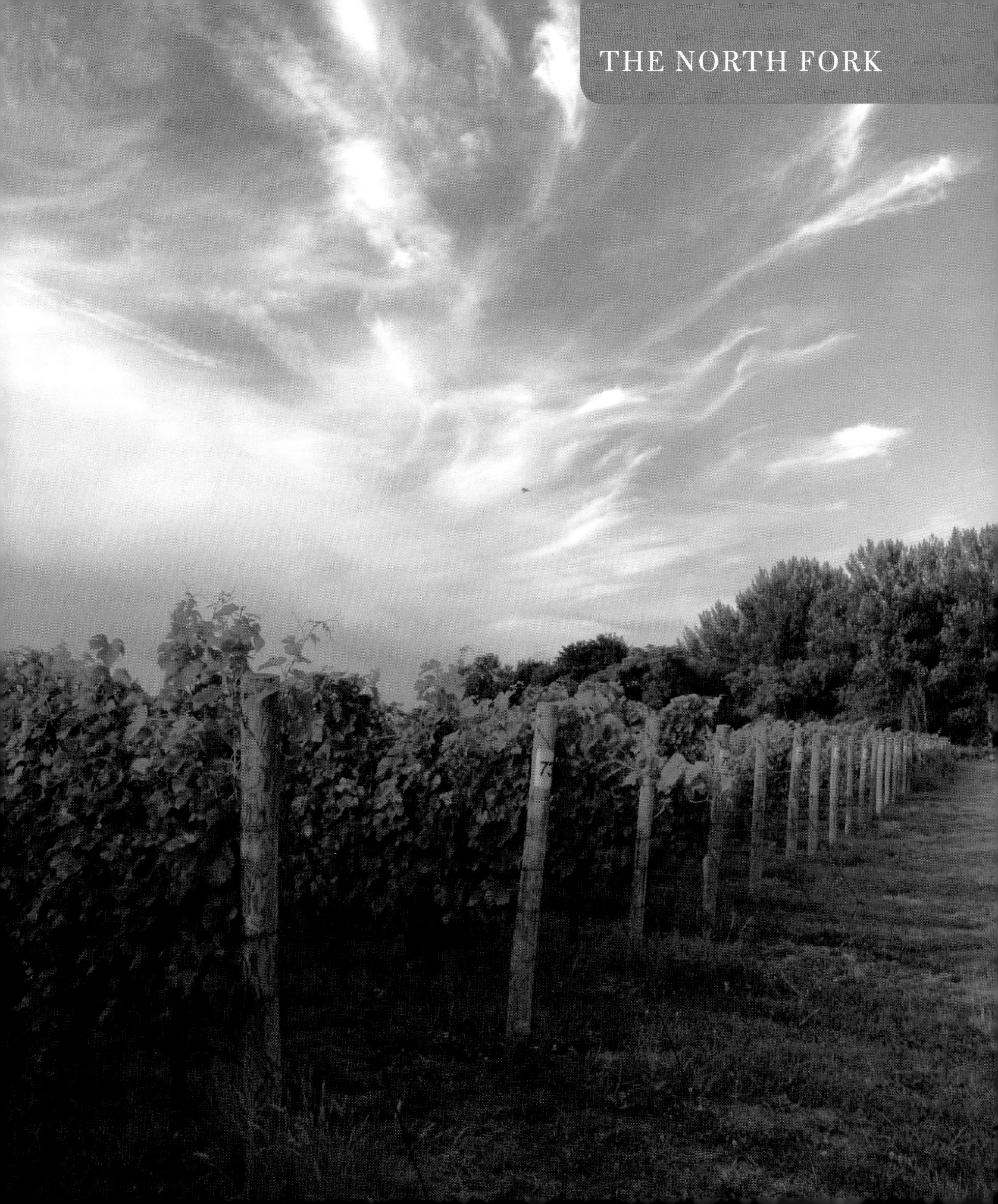

BAITING HOLLOW FARM VINEYARD

ONE OF THE NEWER NORTH FORK VINEYARDS, BAITING HOLLOW FARM VINEYARD IS THE FIRST ONE YOU'LL COME TO IF YOU TAKE EXIT 71 from the Long Island Expressway and go north on Edwards Avenue to Sound Avenue. Turn right and you're almost there. You can't miss the beautifully restored 1861 farmhouse set amid horse paddocks and vineyards.

Enter the tasting room and you'll feel as if you're in an exclusive club or an upscale English pub. With its cozy ambience and friendly staff, this is a tasting room you won't want to leave.

The grounds are equally inviting. Huge old trees cast welcoming shade over a brick-paved patio, and visitors can gaze at the horses beyond the paddock fence while sipping wine on a summer afternoon.

The Owners, the Rubin Family

On a cold and windy Wednesday in January, a guest joins two members of the Rubin family, Sharon Levine and her brother Richard Rubin, in the tasting room at Baiting Hollow Farm Vineyard. Over a glass of Cabernet Franc, they talk about the beginnings of their venture.

"We had owned Weight Watchers of Suffolk for over forty years," Sharon begins, "so we have a business background, and we always thought it would be nice to do something like this, but it was kind of on the back burner. My dad had always been into organic farming; it was a hobby for many years. He always had land upstate and in Vermont, and on weekends he would go up there and do his farming. But once the grandchildren started coming, he decided he wanted to be home a little bit more, because he felt like he was away every weekend. So he said, 'You know, I'm just going to buy something out on the East End.'

"We were all surprised, because we didn't realize there was still farmland out here," she continues. "We never came out here. We'd go out to the Hamptons, but we were never on the North Fork. So he bought the land and we all came out and saw it. It was a dilapidated old house and the barn was awful, but the land was beautiful and it was so nice out here; we just fell in love with it."

That was in 1988. For the first several years, Sam Rubin, the family patriarch, grew enough organic produce to supply his family and friends. Then, in the mid-1990s, he made a fateful decision.

"One day he came home and said, 'You know, I'm going to throw in some grapes,' " Sharon says, "and the next thing you know, he put in a few rows. Everything he grows, he has such a green thumb; it really started to take off, and we planted more and more. Once you have that many grapes, you've got to make wine. Then that segues into, 'Oh, we have to sell it.' And we'd always dreamed of redoing the house and the barn. We ended up being able to open the tasting room, because you need the tasting room to supply that. That was kind of the dream, but it was in the back of our minds because we still

had Weight Watchers, and that was a lot of work."

Richard joins the conversation. "I think one of the things that we're all enjoying is having an opportunity to provide support for my father so that his dreams can be attained. We spent the better part of our lives doing the very same thing with regard to Rhoda Rubin, our mother. We're very proud of her," Richard says. "She built a very big organization in Suffolk County that I think helped countless people. It was always a business that was based upon helping people.

"Now that we're no longer in Weight Watchers," he goes on, "we're able to do the same thing for our father in his lifetime, and we're seeing already the accolades and the results of his hard work and beliefs. It's a very special opportunity very few children get. We've been accustomed to working with one another for more years than we care to admit in Weight Watchers, and we've enjoyed it. Not that there aren't challenges, because there always are if people are honest about being in business, especially a business that you care a lot about and spend a lot of time with. But, you know, we've always been a team."

Clearly passionate about his subject, Richard leans forward as he speaks. "The team now has a

similar purpose, in terms of setting goals and trying to attain those goals for ourselves. We've always taken a lot of pride in that.

"In our training here," he says, "one of the things we talk about is, you leave your problems at the door and remember what it's like when you walk into a vineyard tasting house and how you want to feel validated in choosing that particular place. You want to come in, you want to be greeted with a smile, you want to feel that this is a place where you're welcome, not just once, but many, many times, sort of like a home away from home."

As if to illustrate everything he's been saying, a couple comes in from the wind and cold. Although the tasting room is closed, Sharon and Richard welcome the couple like old friends, offering them

a taste on the house and warmly inviting them to return. No doubt they will.

When it came to learning the ropes of the wine business, Richard went about it with characteristic efficiency. "That's the beauty of getting involved in an area that's known for producing," he says, "because you don't have to reinvent the wheel. You look at what some of the more successful growers are doing and what the market response is, and you learn from that. Certainly we took that into consideration.

"You sort of learn a little as you go along," he adds. "You have to be intelligent and to recognize what you know versus what you don't know, and I think that one of the best ways to make certain you get on a surefooted path is to make sure you have the proper guidance, and you can hire that.

"We hired some really top people, including a great winemaker, Tom Drozd," Richard tells his guest with evident pride. "And we also have Steve Mudd in the vineyard, the top vineyard manager in the industry. I really rely heavily upon those guys. The production is done at the Premium Wine Group. I work very closely with Russell Hearn, who's in charge there. When I look at Russell and Steve and Tom in conjunction with my father, who brings his own inside knowledge, I feel very blessed," he concludes.

If some of the horses in the paddock could talk, they would say they feel blessed, too; the Rubin family saved them from the slaughterhouse. The family has always loved animals, and the purchase of the Baiting Hollow farm sparked the idea to take in rescue horses.

"I had a preliminary meeting with a horse-rescue person, just to find out what was involved," Sharon recalls. "While she was here she got a phone call and she just burst into tears. I said, 'What's the matter?' and she said there was a trailer load of thirty-two horses going to slaughter and she just had to rescue some.

"You have to buy them by the pound from the slaughterhouse," Sharon continues, "and of course she didn't have the money for that, so we rescued five of them. One is a one-and-a-half-year-old Thoroughbred, a little baby! She came in covered in bite marks because the other horses get so agitated in the slaughter pen that they were all attacking the baby.

"We wish we could have saved them all, but you know, you can't," she adds. "We hope eventually we'll be able to take in more, but it's a very, very expensive endeavor. The initial payment was really nothing compared to everything from the trailers to get them here to nursing them back to health and taking care of them. It's been a labor of love. We're going to start boarding horses here to help pay for the horse-rescue operation."

That's the way it seems to be at Baiting Hollow Farm Vineyard. Everything they do is a labor of love, one that involves the whole family. There's a lot of overlap, but in general Richard is the overall manager; Sharon handles marketing and events; their sister Paula Geonie is in charge of public relations and the Web site; Sharon's husband, Steve Levine, manages wholesale wine sales; Richard's wife, Katrina, is the interior decorator and gift buyer; and mom Rhoda Rubin is looked to as a consultant while managing the wine club.

Even the third generation gets involved. "On any given weekend," Sharon says, "you can come in and find my kids pulling cases out of the basement, and Richard's daughter has been baking some of the homemade stuff."

A little while later, Sharon reflects on how far they've come. "It's a totally different life," she says. "A year and a half ago we were dressing in business suits every day, and now it's throw on a pair of boots and a pair of jeans, and it's really fun. It's different." She pauses, then adds with a laugh, "It's like being reinvented at not too young an age!"

As for the patriarch of the clan, Sam Rubin, now past eighty, can still be found working the land he loves and delivering the fruits of his labor to family and friends.

The Wines

The first releases from Baiting Hollow Farm Vineyard were very well received. "People enjoy our wines pretty much across the board," says Richard. "The biggest seller we've had is our Riesling, which

we think is really special." The Riesling is off-dry, fresh and fruity yet complex and balanced, with a palate-pleasing tingle of acidity.

Of the simply named Red Table Wine, Sharon says, "The comments we're getting: 'Oh, my God, you've got to change the name of this wine, it's so fantastic!' " Red Table Wine is a flavorful, easy-drinking, oak-aged blend of 70 percent Cabernet Franc, 25 percent Merlot, and 5 percent Cabernet Sauvignon.

There's a story behind the 2005 Rosé. That year it rained for nine days straight during the last half of harvest. The Rubins' is one of many tales of serendipity arising from near-disaster. Without enough grapes to make a varietal Cabernet Sauvignon, their winemaker came up with a rosé that has become a huge hit. "People are going insane over it," Sharon says. "It almost looks like a red, it's so full-bodied. And that would have never happened if the other thing hadn't happened, so, you know, I guess there are blessings in disguise from time to time."

They've had orders for this unusual wine from as far away as California and from a wine connoisseur who works for a large liquor store. As the story goes, he tasted the wine and told wholesale manager Steve Levine it was the "best rosé anywhere." Sharon enthusiastically continues: "My husband thought he was just being nice, but the next day he got a call at home from the guy, and he said, 'Listen, I'm having a dinner party tomorrow night. You've got to get me a case of this rosé!' "

A rosé made from Merlot is also in the works. The 2007 vintage, which was spectacular all over the East End, will probably result in Baiting Hollow's first premium wine.

Also in the tasting room is a bevy of rich and flavorful reds, including the vineyard's signature Merlot, along with Cabernet Sauvignon, Cabernet Franc, and the aforementioned Red Table Wine.

In whites Baiting Hollow produces a crisp, stainless-steel-fermented Chardonnay and the off-dry Riesling described above.

Baiting Hollow Farm Vineyard
2114 Sound Avenue, Baiting Hollow
(631) 369-0100
info@bhfvineyard.com
www.baitinghollowfarmvineyard.com
Open year-round
Owners: The Rubin family
Winemaker: Tom Drozd
Founded: 1997
Acres planted: 11
Varieties grown: Cabernet Franc, Cabernet Sauvignon, Merlot
Long Island Wine Council member

LOBSTER STEW
Chef John Ross

Stew

    4 1¼-pound lobsters
    2 tablespoons olive oil
    ¼ cup brandy
    1 cup diced onion
    1 tablespoon minced garlic
    1 cup diced leek
    1 cup diced red pepper
    1 cup diced green pepper
    1 sprig fresh thyme
    1 bay leaf
    2 cups heavy cream
    Coarse salt and pepper
    4 ears corn
    8 small, red-skinned potatoes

Herb Butter Garnish

    ¼ pound unsalted butter
    1 teaspoon minced garlic
    1 tablespoon chopped Italian
        parsley, plus more for garnish
    1 tablespoon fresh thyme
    1 tablespoon lemon juice
    Chopped Italian parsley

1. Split the lobsters and remove the claws. Discard the head sacs and scrape out the tomalley and coral into a small bowl. Boil the claws in water until just cooked (about 10 minutes) and set aside.
2. Heat olive oil in a large sauté pan and place the lobster bodies in it, shell side down. Cook until the shells turn red and the meat is opaque. Pour brandy over them and ignite. Remove lobsters from the pan to cool, reserving pan and drippings.
3. Take the meat out of the lobster shells and claws and cut it into bite-size pieces. Place all shells in a pan and cover with water. Bring to a boil and simmer for 30 minutes before straining. Reduce this liquid to about 1 cup.
4. To the pan with the lobster drippings, add diced onion, minced garlic, and diced leek. Sauté until soft and add diced red and green peppers. Add the reduced lobster stock, sprig of thyme, and bay leaf. Simmer until peppers are tender, then add heavy cream. Add coarse salt and pepper to taste and remove from the heat.
5. Shuck corn and grill the ears (over charcoal if possible). Scrape off the kernels and add them to the lobster broth. Boil the potatoes, cut them in half, and add them to the broth. Chop the tomalley and coral and add both to the broth. Bring back to a simmer and add the lobster meat. Hold for service.
6. To make the garnish, soften unsalted butter and add garlic, parsley, thyme, and lemon juice. Stir until combined and mold into a cylinder on a piece of aluminum foil. Wrap the cylinder and refrigerate until firm. At service time, slice into rounds and float them in the stew.
7. Serve the stew in shallow bowls and sprinkle with chopped Italian parsley.

Serves 4. Pair with a full-bodied Long Island Chardonnay.

ROANOKE VINEYARDS

THE SIMPLICITY OF THE CEDAR BOARD–AND–SHINGLE EXTERIOR OF ROANOKE VINEYARDS' TASTING ROOM MAKES AN INTERESTING contrast with its elegant, Old World interior, with its wood-paneled walls, curved tasting bar, and Tiffany-style lamps. At the end of the bar, double glass doors open onto a brick patio overlooking fields and vines, where tables shaded by green canvas umbrellas beckon on a warm summer day. Roanoke is one of those cozy, intimate wineries that, once discovered, becomes an irresistible lure.

The Owner, Richard Pisacano

Everyone who knows Richard Pisacano calls him Richie; its informality suits his generous, down-to-earth manner. One of the most experienced vineyard managers on Long Island, Richie owns Roanoke Vineyards with his wife, Soraya.

In the tasting room early on a chilly November morning, Richie tells a visitor how Roanoke Vineyards arose from his love of green and growing things.

"My passion for this business extends from the aspect of growing something," he begins. "When we

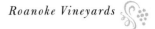

moved out here from Huntington in the late 1960s, my father started a huge garden. He was raised Old World: You ate what you grew. So when we moved out here, we always had this huge garden. It was really impressive, because at any given time it was about five times what you could actually eat. And it was fun; moving out to Southold was a change of environment and culture.

"I think for the most part that's where my interest grew: being around agriculture in this new area, potatoes as far as you can see, and working on vegetable farms as a thirteen-year-old," Richie continues. "One of my first jobs was picking brussels sprouts. And maybe also it was the greenhouse operations that were just starting up. That was something that kind of grew my passion for growing things. There's just something about being around farmers that ingrains something in your spirit, in your personality."

While he was in high school, Richie worked for the Mudds, the area's most respected vineyardists. He was still working for them when he started at Suffolk County Community College, where he took a course in greenhouse management along with his general studies.

"My plan was to move on and be a greenhouse producer," he says. "I think probably the change of heart came when we learned grafting at Mudd Vineyards, grapevine propagation. It's what drew me back into the vineyard business and made me stay: the idea of producing great vines and becoming a nursery for this new industry."

He was twenty-one when he bought twelve acres in Jamesport and planted seven of them with Chardonnay vines he had propagated. "My intention was never to open a winery at that point. We were selling grapes to all the new wineries," Richie says.

"In the late 1980s," he continues, "we produced house wines for some restaurants, and that's what started all this. That was exciting. I went one night to talk about the next vintage, and I walked into the restaurant, and just about every table had a bottle of our wine on it. So that was a little dose of what it's like to see people enjoying the specific wine that you produced."

Richie thinks he had an advantage, coming into the wine business knowing what the work was like, not harboring unrealistic, romantic notions. "We came into the business with our eyes wide open, with a clear understanding of most of the hardships, but were still willing to move forward," he says. "There were a handful of others who also understood it, because they grew up in agriculture or were in it long enough to know before they made the next step."

And yet the idealization of winemaking is hard to avoid, as Richie admits. "When I think about

wine and winemaking, I still see the vision of myself under an arbor, but I rarely do it. It's still the image you have in your mind of what the business is about: sharing wines with people, enjoying wines with people, striving to make great wines, bringing the region to its utmost potential. But the reality is, very little of your time is spent doing those things.

"I think that's a big part of what lures people into this industry," he adds. "They visit a region, and they usually visit the sleepy end of it, the relaxing aspect of it, where you go to a tasting or you go to Napa or Tuscany or France, and there's hardly anybody around, and you just see these vines ripening and

you think, 'Well, this is just a beautiful thing; I want to be part of this.' Behind the scenes there's a lot of components, a lot of people working very hard."

By the mid-1990s all of the fruit from his Jamesport vineyard was going to Wölffer Estate Vineyard in the Hamptons, and Richie had established a relationship with Wölffer's winemaker, Roman Roth.

"Roman asked me around Christmastime, I think it was mid-December, 'Why don't you come over and we'll meet and discuss the 1997 vintage?'" Richie recounts, "which was a little odd in retrospect, since you usually waited until late winter or early spring to discuss grapes or grapevines. It turned out to be a job offer."

After careful consideration Richie decided to accept Roman's offer, and he's been the vineyard manager at Wölffer Estate since the end of 1996.

Richie picks up the story a few years later. "Then in—I guess it was '99—still with no intention of getting into the wine business, I was starting to see a conceptual idea of how it would unfold, and that was to think small, which was 180 degrees from what was taking place at the time. It was still, 'Build a grand winery and plant as many acres as possible.'

"I started to think what probably makes more sense is to just do it almost for yourself and start very small; don't have these illusions of grandeur in terms of volume."

The land that became Roanoke Vineyards used to be an apple orchard, Richie says. "It's the footprint of Youngs' Farm. It's a place I had admired as a kid. It was just a neat little place, and I bought it in 2000.

"I was still unsure about the industry and how to move forward," he goes on, "but I wanted to plant reds. It was a great site for the production of reds, so I sort of set the stage for myself or somebody else to go forward with it, with the thought that it can be run by a few people, from making the wine to caring for the vineyard. And then, once the vines were in the ground, that was the hook. When I saw the farm starting to evolve, that's when we knew what we were going to do, where we were going to go with it.

"I think the real deciding factor was when my wife, Soraya, who was working for Southampton Town at the time—I asked her if that was something she wanted to be a part of, wanted to pursue, and she said yes, and she helped from the ground up in terms of the planning and the licensing," Richie

relates. "That's when I got into it, because I knew that without her support, or somebody else kind of being the nucleus of the business, it would require finding somebody and going into it on a different level. That's when I said, 'Let's do it,' which she's done with great success."

The Wines

Roman Roth makes Roanoke's wines in consultation with Richie. "I think the style was a spark from the great region that we admire, Bordeaux, the Old World," Richie explains. "The basic philosophy is minimal intervention in the winery. These are wines that can be made in the most rustic wineries, using your feet. And it's always been Roman's direction to make wines with longevity, true to the style and the region.

"The difference between red and white wine that makes it so exciting for me," Richie adds, "is making a wine that has a long life, a long evolution, that will change in the glass as you're enjoying it and wait for you. When you're ready for a red, it will be ready for you, as opposed to a white wine, which you may have to open because it's time."

Richie recalls Roanoke Vineyards' first Merlot. "The first lot was picked, then it got crushed and brought into the tank. And what was very impressive was Roman's excitement for that tank and what was in it. He protected and hovered over that tank, and seeing that just got me super excited about it.

"We had been fermenting some Cabernet Sauvignon," Richie continues, "and that became a very special wine that we made a varietal Cabernet Sauvignon from. It was kind of neat to see this wine evolve that was made basically in a plastic box—a bin, they're called. It sort of supported the notion that a great wine can be made using very basic

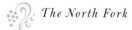
equipment. And that wine turned out to be put on the "highly recommended" list in *Wine Spectator*, the 2003 Cabernet Sauvignon.

"So it was a great year. Our first Cabernet got 88 points and was put on the list of highly recommended new releases from New York. The second release won Best Red Wine at the New York Wine and Food Classic, and the third was highly regarded by David Schildknecht in *Wine Advocate*," Richie says, referring to a critic from the respected wine newsletter. "Everybody's making great wines now," he adds. "The bar's getting lifted, and we hope to keep clearing it."

Roanoke's reds include Merlot, Cabernet Sauvignon, and two Bordeaux-style blends called Blend One and Blend Two. A stainless-steel- and barrel-fermented Chardonnay and an off-dry rosé called De Rosa round out the wine list.

As of this writing, all of Roanoke Vineyards' wines are sold only in the tasting room or through the Web site; they tend to sell out quickly.

Roanoke Vineyards
3543 Sound Avenue, Riverhead
(631) 727-4161
info@roanokevineyards.com
www.roanokevineyards.com
Open year-round
Owners: Richard and Soraya Pisacano
Winemaker: Roman Roth
Founded: 2000
Acres planted: 10
Varieties grown: Cabernet Franc, Cabernet Sauvignon, Merlot
Long Island Wine Council member

PALMER VINEYARDS

PALMER VINEYARDS' WINERY HAS THE LOOK OF A STREAMLINED, CONTEMPORARY FARMHOUSE. THERE'S SOMETHING SOOTHING ABOUT THE sleek lines of its silvered wood, cleanly gabled windows, and peaked roof. Inside, you may take a self-guided tour, looking down into the winery through large windows. At the end of the tour, a door takes you outside, where a brick walkway leading to the tasting house bisects a lawn set with picnic tables and Adirondack chairs.

The tasting house is a British-style pub, with wide-plank flooring, tall tasting tables, a long bar, and three booths with tables, benches, and Tiffany-style hanging lamps.

The best view of the vineyard is from the spacious deck, whose pillars, roof beams, and railings have been painted pristine white, lending it a gracious Southern charm.

The Owner, Robert Palmer, and Winemaker, Miguel Martin

Over lunch and a glass of Palmer Vineyards Chardonnay, Bob Palmer and his winemaker, Miguel Martin, talk about where they came from and how they ended up on the North Fork, growing grapes and making wine. Physically, the two are opposites: Where Bob is tall and imposing, with light hair, Miguel is compact and trim, with the dark hair of his Spanish heritage.

"I was born on Long Island," Bob begins, then qualifies that statement with a chuckle. "I was born in Queens, which counts, and I live in Huntington. Most of my business background is in advertising, the television end of advertising.

"For most of my career I had an office in San Francisco," he says later, "and for a good part of my career, I had an apartment there. You can't go to San Francisco without being hounded by wine people. They take you to wine bars, private wine clubs; they make you go to Napa Valley; they talk wine; they live wine. And I knew nothing, I mean nothing! Eventually I discovered I was the only one back here

in my circle of friends who knew anything about wine, so I said, hey, this is pretty good!"

After he sold one of his advertising agencies, Bob began to pay attention to the stories he was hearing about vineyards on Long Island. "I'd been reading about the Hargraves, of course," he recounts, "and there was an article in the *New York Times* about Dave Mudd. It said he could manage the vineyard and plant for you, and so that was a piece of the puzzle I didn't have. . . . I was just going to have a vineyard, but Dave kept pushing me to do the winery, so after about a year, a year and a half, I finally decided to do a winery.

"We bought the property in December of 1982," he continues, "and we planted in the spring of '83. Our first crop was '85, which was Hurricane Gloria; most of the crop was floating out in Long Island Sound. So we made a minor bit of wine in

'85, which we kept very quiet, and '86 we call our first vintage. That year we won the top medal in the state for Chardonnay. That sort of gave us a nice leg up and a good name from the get-go."

Miguel Martin has been Palmer Vineyards' winemaker since September 2006, but he started making wine on the East End long before that. "I'm not from Long Island like Bob is, as you can probably tell by my accent," Miguel says with a mischievous smile. "I came to Long Island in 1989, looking for experience to work in the wine industry. I found a job working at a winery in the Hamptons; it was called Le Rêve." That winery eventually became Duck Walk Vineyards.

"I became the first winemaker there," Miguel continues. "I felt Long Island was very unique, very special. That was still the beginning of the Long Island wine country. There were only a few wineries, and the people were still deciding about what to grow, what wines to make, how to make them.

"After that I went to UC Davis." Miguel says. "I got my master's degree there, and after twelve years in California, after September 11, I had an opportunity to go back to Spain to work in a winery, to build a brand-new winery—a huge winery, 1.4 million cases of wine—from the ground up. It was a challenge I thought I would never be able to accomplish, because opportunities like that only come once in a lifetime. So we took the chance and moved with the family to Spain, and we were there for almost three years."

"You might want to mention that you married a local girl," Bob interjects.

Miguel smiles and nods. "Yep. My wife, Ellen, is from Southampton. She always thought, 'Ah, it would be so wonderful if we could come back to where you started in Long Island, and I would be close to my father and my sisters.' And, sure enough, I was

checking the Internet and there was a job posting at Palmer Vineyards, so I presented my résumé and I got hired, and we moved from Spain to here. And here I am, working for one of the original wineries in Long Island. We couldn't be any happier. It certainly has been a good move.

"Long Island is very unique," Miguel goes on. "I've been all over the world—I worked in Chile, Australia, California—and I have to tell you that this is a place that you cannot rest, thinking you have done everything in your life, because every year tests your skills. Every year is different; every year you don't know if it's going to be hot, or humid, or rainy, or if the Merlot is going to ripen faster than the Cabernet Franc, or the Cabernet Franc's going to be delayed, or the Cabernet Sauvignon's never going to get ripe. You can get rain in the middle of the harvest. It's really very challenging to make wine here."

"Long Island can compete with any major wine region in the world," Miguel says a little later. "Sure, we'll never have the 14½-to-15 percent alcohol Chardonnays. We don't have the heat; we don't have the sunshine that California has. In California it's going to be 90 degrees, 95 degrees or 105. Here, it's like, 'Oh geez, is it gonna rain? Oh, I don't know, it's half a degree colder or warmer than yesterday. Well, that's good.' But here you have more aromatic, natural flavors. You don't have the intensity, but you have a lot of finesse. The same thing in France. They don't have the sunshine they have in California, and they produce wonderful wines. Or Germany, with the Riesling."

Miguel was born in Cordova, Spain, and grew up in Madrid. "My father, he always drank wine for lunch and dinner. The first thing my mother did when she was setting the table was to put on a bottle of wine. Before bread, silverware, anything. A bare table, a bottle of wine.

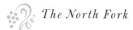

"Nowadays everybody's worried about what do you eat, how do you cook," Miguel adds. "There's a lot more magazines about food and wine and travel, and to me it's all part of the same thing. If you start thinking about how much emphasis you put on what you eat, you should put an emphasis on what you drink. And wine is to me one of the complements you can have to your meal."

A big part of Palmer Vineyards' mission is to make wines that appeal to people at all levels of wine knowledge and appreciation, not just those Bob calls "wine snobs."

"We're trying to attract people who will accept that wine is a valid beverage, and then, when they come in, start with training wheels," he says. "Our two best sellers at the winery are training-wheel wines. They're somewhat sweet—a sweet white and now a sweet red—and that's fine. Guests can try that

and gradually build their palate up. I think that does everybody a service."

Miguel agrees. "We say, 'Well, have this wine with pasta, or with pizza, or with cheese.' It doesn't need to be with something so sophisticated. But you start appreciation of the wines. You start with the rosé, you start with the whites, then we go with the light reds, and before you know it, you start tasting red wines that awhile ago you never thought you could taste."

Bob and Miguel see also see eye to eye on the vital role of vineyard management. "I love to spend time in the vineyard, because really it's when you can make a difference in how the wine is going to turn out," says Miguel. "When you harvest the grapes and you bring the grapes to the winery, you don't have to say, 'Oh, I wish I could leave the grapes hanging for a week, or two days, or five days.' You need to go in the vineyard, taste the fruit, and make those decisions based on what you are tasting. I don't make wine by the book. I consider myself a winegrower as well."

"I travel with him through the vineyard sometimes, and I see what he's doing," Bob adds. "And it's nice—we have two vineyards, so we have enough acreage to isolate certain spots for this or that. We have four or five different Chardonnay stands, and then this year we're just coming out with another six acres of new plants that are ready to be picked for the first time. It will be interesting where we go with that."

Bob draws on his experience in advertising to dream up creative promotions for Palmer Vineyards. "I can't make wine," he says, "and we have so many wines in the tasting room, I get confused if I try to work behind the bar. But I can sell, and I come up with all these promotions we do."

As a result of Bob's efforts, his wine is the official wine of the Yankees and Mets radio networks, and there's a deal in the works involving the Mets farm team, the Brooklyn Cyclones. Palmer wine is sold in various venues across the country, including ABC Fine Wines & Spirits, the largest chain of alcoholic beverage stores in the United States. Palmer Vineyards makes private-label wines for such well-known restaurants as Fulton's Crab House at Disney World and Gallagher's Steak House, which has franchises across the country. Palmer's private-label wines are also served in a number of well-known New York City restaurants, including the View.

Bob sees to it that Palmer Vineyards is a place where families feel welcome, where people can come and have a good time while enjoying good wine. As he describes a promotion run jointly with Long Island's daily newspaper, *Newsday*, pride swells in his voice.

"*Newsday* ran a contest, the prize being coming here for a tour that we gave," Bob recounts. "And for the first time I got letters from people, thanking me. One of the things they said to me was, 'This is the most relaxed place I've ever been to.' "

The Wines

Palmer Vineyards produces about fifteen thousand cases of wine each year. Recent awards include three silver and five bronze medals for Cabernet Franc, and a bronze medal for N41/W72 Merlot Cuvée (named for the North Fork's latitude and longitude).

Whites on the wine list at this writing are House White, Sauvignon Blanc, Lighthouse White, Gewürztraminer, Reserve Chardonnay, N41/W72 Chardonnay, Pinot Blanc, and White Riesling. Palmer's Sparkling Brut is made from Chardonnay and Pinot Blanc by the traditional Champagne method.

The reds: House Red, Merlot, Cabernet Franc, N41/W72 Merlot Cuvée, Cabernet Sauvignon, and Lighthouse Red.

Palmer Vineyards
5120 Sound Avenue, Riverhead
(631) 722-9463
palmervineyards@mail.com
www.palmervineyards.com
Open year-round
Owner: Robert Palmer
Winemaker: Miguel Martin
Founded: 1986
Acres planted: 125
Varieties grown: Chardonnay, Riesling, Gewürztraminer, Pinot Blanc, Sauvignon Blanc, Cabernet Franc, Cabernet Sauvignon, Merlot
Long Island Wine Council member

MARTHA CLARA VINEYARDS

ARTHA CLARA VINEYARDS IS A WINERY WITH A DIFFERENCE, AND THAT DIFFERENCE IS EVIDENT FROM THE MOMENT YOU arrive. In a paddock right on Sound Avenue, on any given day you might see Scottish Highland cattle, donkeys, or llamas grazing. Behind the cedar-shingled, barnlike building that houses a gift shop, expansive tasting room, and enclosed patio, a spacious pen is home to a few sheep, contentedly cropping the grass. And guests can climb aboard a wagon pulled by two handsome Percherons for a tour through the 112-acre vineyard.

There's a demonstration kitchen in the glass-walled patio and another in a separate building out back. Two barns have been restored and turned into art galleries. Art shows, live music, cooking demonstrations, wine and beer festivals, and myriad other special events are a big draw for all ages.

The Owners, Robert Entenmann and Jacqueline Entenmann Damianos

Martha Clara Vineyards started out to be the retirement home of Robert Entenmann, one of three sons of the founders of the famous Entenmann's

Bakery. After the business was sold, Robert bought a potato farm and turned it into a Thoroughbred horse farm. "We were into horses," he tells a visitor. "We went all the way and bred Thoroughbreds. At one time my family had two hundred mares. After you do that for a while, you look for something else."

Robert's daughter and partner in the business, Jacqueline Entenmann Damianos, laughs. "This is a man who sailed around the world," she says. "What do you do to top that?"

The "something else" Robert was looking for became Martha Clara Vineyards, named for his mother, who was the benevolent force behind the family bakery business after her husband died. It was Martha Clara's inspired idea to make the top of Entenmann boxes transparent, as they still are today.

"I looked around, and everybody was planting a vineyard," says Robert. "It looked like it would be fun."

Jackie chimes in: "We like to have fun, and we've cultivated a fun atmosphere. We want people to be relaxed when they come here."

"We always had animals anyway," adds Robert, "half a zoo sometimes. And people love it. They bring their kids to feed the animals, and they taste the wine."

Robert worked in his family's business, but Jackie went far afield to find a career she expected to stay with long-term. "I worked in politics in the city," she says, "and I really enjoyed it. And I worked on Capitol Hill. But I just got tired of doing the New York City grind, riding the subway and everything. So when my dad said he was planting a vineyard and asked me if I'd like to be part of it, I said, 'Heck, yeah!' " A stint at culinary school seemed to fit right in with her new plans. "It was a natural progression," Jackie says.

To learn the ropes she worked at a winery in

Westport, Massachusetts. "I was a tour guide, I worked behind the tasting bar; I did whatever they asked me to do, and I'm indebted to them."

The experience has served her well in managing the day-to-day operations of the business.

As for Robert, he loves to go out among the vines and check the grapes. "I really like the vineyards," he says. "That, to me, is everything. I check to see that the clusters are dangling by themselves the way they should be, that there's not too many clusters; I check the sugar—a lot of things. You can get an idea just by walking through the vineyard. It's a lot more work than people would ever imagine."

He smiles at vineyard manager Wojtek Majewski, who has joined the conversation. "Ripeness is the whole thing, right?" Robert asks rhetorically, and Wojtek concurs with a nod and a smile.

Jackie's excited about getting more involved in winemaking. "I'm really ready to jump in. It's the only way I'm going to learn, you know—get in there and do it. Being with Jason, I'm learning a lot more."

Jackie is talking about her husband, Jason Damianos, son of "Dr. Dan" Damianos, whose family owns and operates Pindar, Duck Walk, and Duck Walk North. Jason and Jackie eloped to Las Vegas in January 2007. Jason has his own small vineyard on the Main Road in Jamesport and is building a winery and tasting room there.

The Winemaker, Juan Micieli-Martinez

"I was born in Mexico, then adopted and raised on Long Island," says Juan Micieli-Martinez, known as John. He spent time on the East End during the

Chef Michael Anthony (left), bayman Timmy Hermus, and chef David Girard demonstrate oyster shucking at Martha Clara Vineyards.

summers and watched with interest as the vineyards expanded and multiplied. After graduating with a dual degree in biology and psychology, he planned to go into biotechnology and pharmaceuticals, but his plans changed.

"I wanted to take one last summer job to learn about wine," he says. He worked with master winemaker Russell Hearn at Pellegrini Vineyards. "A position opened up in the laboratory, where they run lab analyses on the wines," John recounts. "One day, I'm grabbing samples out in the vineyard, and it was like, 'I think I can do this for a living.' " He jokes that he's still working his last summer job.

John then pursued winemaking experience locally and abroad. "I worked a vintage in Australia, and I traveled around a bit to other wine regions."

Asked about his approach to winemaking, John replies: "Most winemakers say wine is made in the vineyard, but how many do you see out there on a daily basis? I try to be out in the vineyard every day, looking at the grapes, communicating with the vineyard manager, really being proactive in the vineyard, because when you do that, it makes your job easier in the winery."

In Australia John learned about a technique he's putting into practice at Martha Clara. "I got to see a lot of anaerobic winemaking," he says, "winemaking in the absence of oxygen. The idea with that, especially with aromatic white varietals, is that oxygen will degrade the aromas. And you use very cool fermentation, all in an effort to retain as much aromatics as possible."

John is big on blending, too. "I like the idea of blends," he says. "You can blend different varietals that aren't traditionally put together. It's fun as a winemaker, because anaerobic winemaking, cold

and Syrah. Red and white blends have become a specialty here. An impressive array in both categories—varietals and blends—has earned high praise and numerous medals. From 2005 to early 2008, Martha Clara wines won a double gold, four gold, and twenty-three silver medals in prestigious international competitions.

Currently on the wine list are twenty-six wines in a number of different styles, including dry, nuanced Bordeaux-style red blends like 6025 and Five-O Red; complex white blends like Five-O White; sweeter quaffers like Red Sweetie and Sabor; dessert wines like the nectary Himmel; and zesty sparklers in three styles.

Varietal wines include Pinot Grigio, Riesling, Chardonnay, Gewürztraminer, Viognier, Merlot, Cabernet Sauvignon, Syrah, Cabernet Franc, and Pinot Noir.

fermentation, that's science. It's interesting, but it can be boring at times, whereas when you're putting in 10 percent of this and that and coming up with these blends, that's the real art of winemaking and the fun part. It's the exciting part as well. I like the idea of blending whites, too. Chardonnay, Viognier, Sauvignon Blanc, Semillon—you don't typically see all these things put together, and the outcome of doing that is something like Martha Clara's Five-O," a blend of six red varietals. "It's exciting and interesting to do."

The Wines

More than a dozen varieties of grapes are grown at Martha Clara Vineyards. The wines, produced at Premium Wine Group, include varietals relatively rare in the region, such as Semillon, Viognier,

Martha Clara Vineyards
6025 Sound Avenue, Riverhead
(631) 298-0075
info@marthaclaravineyards.com
www.marthaclaravineyards.com
Open year-round
Owners: Robert Entenmann and Jacqueline Entenmann Damianos
Head winemaker: Juan Micieli-Martinez
Founded: 1995
Acres planted: 200
Major varieties grown: Chardonnay, Gewürztraminer, Riesling, Semillon, Viognier, Cabernet Franc, Cabernet Sauvignon, Merlot, Syrah
Long Island Wine Council member

STRAWBERRY-RHUBARB COBBLER WITH ROSE CREAM

The North Fork Table & Inn, Southold | *Claudia Fleming, pastry chef*

Cobbler Dough

1⅔ cups all-purpose flour

3½ tablespoons sugar

1½ tablespoons baking powder

⅛ teaspoon salt

2 hard-boiled egg yolks

6 tablespoons (3 ounces) very cold
    unsalted butter, cut into ½-inch
    pieces

⅔ cup plus 2 tablespoons very cold
    heavy cream

Strawberry-Rhubarb Filling

¾ cup granulated sugar

1-inch piece vanilla bean, split, with
    pulp scraped

½ pound strawberries

1½ pounds rhubarb, trimmed and
    cut into 1-inch pieces

2½ tablespoons cornstarch

1 teaspoon rosewater (optional)

2 tablespoons turbinado sugar

Rose Cream

1 cup crème fraîche

¼ cup rose preserves

1. In the bowl of a food processor, combine flour, sugar, baking powder, salt, and egg yolks. Pulse to combine until yolks are broken down. Add butter and mix until dough resembles fine meal. Add ⅔ cup cream and pulse until dough just comes together.

2. Turn dough out onto a lightly floured board and gently gather it into a mass (the dough needn't be smooth). Using a large spoon dipped in flour, form dough into 8 to 10 balls, each 2 inches in diameter. Chill for 30 minutes to 8 hours.

3. In a small bowl combine sugar and vanilla bean; mix until the vanilla bean is dispersed evenly in the sugar (you can use your fingers).

4. In a large bowl toss together the strawberries, rhubarb, cornstarch, rosewater, and vanilla sugar. Allow to macerate for 20 minutes.

5. Preheat oven to 350°F. Put the strawberry-rhubarb filling in a shallow 2½-quart baking dish. Flatten dough balls into biscuits and arrange them on top, leaving approximately 1 inch between them. Brush the biscuits with the 2 remaining tablespoons of cream and sprinkle with the turbinado sugar.

6. Bake the cobbler until the fruit is bubbling and the biscuits are golden brown, 30–40 minutes.

7. Beat the crème fraîche in the bowl of an electric mixer on medium-high speed until it thickens. Add the preserves and whip until stiff peaks form.

8. Serve cobbler in a shallow bowl with a dollop of rose cream.

Serves 8–10.

COMTESSE THÉRÈSE

ON TEN UNDULATING ACRES IN AQUEBOGUE, THERESA DILWORTH AND HER HUSBAND, MINEO "SAMMY" SHIMURA, OVERSEE THEIR vineyard, which is densely planted in Cabernet Sauvignon, Merlot, Pinot Grigio, and Sauvignon Blanc. Sammy, a certified sommelier who was a steel-industry CEO in his former life, is the full-time vineyard manager. Theresa, an international tax attorney for pharmaceutical giant Pfizer Inc., spends the workweek in Manhattan.

In the middle of a hot, dry August, two visitors drove to the end of a dusty road to find Theresa dressed in cutoff denim overalls, well-worn work boots, and a wide-brimmed straw hat. Sammy, wearing a white hazmat suit, sat astride a tractor fitted with a spraying apparatus. He got down to meet the guests; then, with the grapes ripening fast under a brilliant blue sky, he climbed back aboard and continued his work in a distant part of the vineyard.

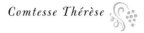

David Dilworth, Theresa's father, is a philosophy professor at Stony Brook University. He and her mother, who is Japanese, can often be found working among the vines on weekends.

Comtesse Thérèse wines are made to Theresa's specifications at Premium Wine Group's custom-crush facility in Mattituck.

The Owner and Winemaker, Theresa Dilworth

Theresa has two partners, Japanese businesswomen Chizuko Tomita and Kayomi Hirota, making Comtesse Thérèse, as of this writing, the only all female-owned vineyard in New York State.

Theresa is a Long Island native who grew up in Lloyd Harbor. "I've always lived on Long Island," she says. "I was born here and I never plan to live anywhere else." When they came to the North Fork, Theresa and Sammy built their own house in Mattituck.

She credits the family garden with inspiring her love for the land. "My parents always had very big gardens," she says. "When I was a kid I was always out with the plants—vegetables, flowers, fruit. But farming is very different from gardening; it takes a huge amount of money."

"Another thing I love is real estate—land," Theresa adds. "Constructing a vineyard is very architectural. You're taking the land and making it into something. But it's good to have both the city life, with a big corporation, and the contrast of a small business and farms. It's very entrepreneurial, very much of a contrast inside and out. It's good to have both city and country."

There's another vital part of Theresa's world: food. "I really love food and cooking," she says. "One hobby I never get tired of is cooking dinner, making things taste good. Wine fits in with that."

Theresa Dilworth harvests Merlot grapes at her Aquebogue vineyard.

Theresa says all of the things she loves add up to something complex and wonderful. "All of these things come together in the vineyard: art, culture, history, climate, soil, people, personal tastes. It's a kaleidoscope of so many things. It's so interesting, so rich, and it's constantly changing—all the little bits and pieces."

The Wines

Comtesse Thérèse produced wine from purchased fruit for six vintages—2001 to 2006. Those early efforts, with output starting at five hundred and fifty cases and topping out at twelve hundred, earned numerous awards, including Best Merlot at the 2004 New York Wine and Food Classic. Since 2005 small bottlings have been produced at the vineyard from estate-grown grapes, but most of the wine is still produced at Premium Wine Group.

Theresa, who made wine and beer at home for several years and spent time observing viticultural techniques in France, is head winemaker. She works with consultant winemaker Bernard Cannac, a native of France whose family owns several vineyards there.

Rather than inoculating with commercially available yeast to begin the fermentation process, Theresa allows the wild, indigenous yeasts that occur naturally on grape skins to accomplish fermentation. After six to eighteen months of barrel aging, the reds are bottled without filtering or fining, two commonly used practices that remove tiny solid particles from the wine and clarify its color. The Chardonnay is 100 percent barrel fermented, also with wild yeasts, in Russian or mixed Russian and French barrels. Comtesse Thérèse is unusual in the region in using Hungarian, Russian, and Canadian oak in addition to French and American.

Another thing that sets Comtesse Thérèse apart is its focus on Cabernet Sauvignon. This grape can be very difficult to ripen in eastern Long Island's relatively cool climate, but Theresa points to her sunny hillside and the location of her vineyard—more inland and farther west than many of the others, making for a slightly longer growing season—as reasons for her firm commitment to this noble Bordeaux varietal.

Comtesse Thérèse currently offers several different styles of red varietals and blends that consistently receive praise from wine critics. They include Cabernet Sauvignon, Traditional Merlot, Hungarian Oak Merlot, Chateau Reserve Merlot, and a Cabernet Franc/Cabernet Sauvignon blend. Completing the list are Rosé, Blanc de Noir, and Russian Oak Chardonnay. These wines are available at the Tasting Room in Peconic.

Comtesse Thérèse
(631) 871-9194
www.comtessetherese.com
Primary owner and winemaker: Theresa Dilworth
Consulting winemaker: Bernard Cannac
Founded: 2000
Acres planted: 10
Varieties grown: Pinot Grigio, Sauvignon Blanc, Cabernet Sauvignon, Merlot
Long Island Wine Council member
Tastings at the Tasting Room
Peconic Lane, Peconic
(631) 765-6404
mail@tastingroomli.com
www.tastingroomli.com
Open year-round

Paumanok Vineyards

At college in 1968, the same year she met Charles, her future husband, Ursula Winter discovered the poetry of Walt Whitman, a native of Long Island, who called his birthplace "my beloved Paumanok." Fifteen years later, when the couple founded their vineyard and winery, the name was a natural fit.

Paumanok Vineyards can't be seen from the road. It's not until you pull into the parking lot that you catch your first glimpse of the renovated hundred-year-old barn that houses the tasting and tank rooms, winery, and barrel cellar. Vertical cedar boards, silvered by time and weather, are crisply accented by white-framed windows and barn doors faced with white, X-shaped beams.

The grounds are lushly landscaped with flowering shrubs and evergreens. Redbrick walkways lead visitors to the tasting room entrance and a wraparound deck, where hanging baskets burgeon with fragrant flowers. Inside, the first thing you'll notice, through a pyramid of windows, is the vineyard stretching into the distance. From midsummer to early fall, red, white, and yellow roses set off the green vines.

The Owners, Charles and Ursula Massoud

At first glance it seems that Charles and Ursula Massoud have come a long way from their origins. Charles was born into a family of hoteliers and restaurateurs in Lebanon, and Ursula was born in Germany, where her family had been making wine and beer for generations. But if you combine their backgrounds in hospitality and winemaking, it's pretty clear that these two apples haven't fallen far from their respective trees after all.

"My father didn't have a farm," Charles recalls, "but he had a very large orchard and, when he went to visit his mother, they also had some orchards in that little village where she lived, so I grew up in an environment where we harvested something. We used to harvest lots of different fruits, and we had in our backyard all the vegetables people grow: lettuce and parsley and mint and cucumbers and tomatoes and squashes—all of those things. So the memories are of extremely good-tasting stuff which was fresh and ripe on the vines, and perhaps you would say some of that carried over. Even before, in my youth, when I was going to school, I always dreamed of farming. I liked the outdoors; I liked the open space."

Ursula talks about her husband's fascination with growing things. "When Charles first came home to meet my family in Germany, it was really pretty amazing, because there was this saying, 'Where's Charles?' He was either out in the vineyard or in the cellar, and he was like a sponge, absorbing everything: 'How do you do this?' 'When do you do this?' Or, when we went to France, I remember our trip to Burgundy. Nobody was out in the vineyard, but he spotted a guy who was pruning. He would spot the guys out in the vineyard, and he would walk in and talk to them."

For Ursula, it was growing up in a family connected to the land that instilled in her an abiding love for growing things. Pointing to several small etchings of rural scenes hanging on the tasting room wall, she says, "This was my childhood in Germany—being out in the vineyard, smelling the barrels, tasting the fermenting cheese, getting excited about bud break—you know, that whole rhythm which goes on in the vineyard, and this whole cycle of rebirth every year, and then the culmination of the intense work in the vineyard that is harvest, when you bring the fruit in, and all the

emotional roller coasters that go on, because, you know, your big partner in all this is Mother Nature.

"It's that mysterious connection not everyone has," she says. "It's passion. It's just a very connected feeling. It's what I tell people when I take them out in the vineyard. You know, we're all part of this—on a very abstract, big level—this web of life."

But Charles and Ursula took a roundabout route to Paumanok Vineyards. He was a sales and marketing executive with IBM. In the 1970s his job took him to Kuwait, where he and Ursula discovered that the Kuwaiti government banned alcoholic beverages. Determined to enjoy wine with their meals, they followed the example of their fellow expatriates and began making their own with table grapes grown in Iraq or grape juice from the supermarket.

"I squeezed the first grapes with my bare knuckles," Charles recalls, "and they were so bruised that when I went to work, someone asked me since when was I doing karate!"

Having their own vineyard was "something of a romantic idea," says Charles. They very much enjoyed their visits with Ursula's family in Germany and wanted that lifestyle for themselves. "As contrasted to the corporate lifestyle, it looked like a great way to transition into something smaller and more tangible," Charles says.

They were drawn by a romantic ideal of vineyard life, but the work itself has proved to be more satisfying than they ever imagined. "The best part is that our children are similarly passionate," says Charles.

The three Massoud sons, Salim, Kareem, and Nabeel, all work full-time in the family business.

Salim, the eldest, pitches in wherever he's needed, making deliveries, helping out in the tasting room, climbing on the tractor, maintaining equipment, and helping with administrative tasks. Nabeel, the youngest son, manages the vineyards, and middle son Kareem has grown into the job of winemaker, working with his father.

It was far from a foregone conclusion that the three Massoud sons would join the family business. In fact, Salim and Kareem, who were old enough be given chores in the new vineyard, weren't exactly thrilled about the weekly trip from their home in Stamford, Connecticut.

"When we first started in 1983, I hated it," says Salim. "There was a long drive, and my parents would put us to work in the vineyard."

"Then we started liking it a little bit more when my dad bought a three-wheeler," Salim continues, smiling at the memory. "We'd ride all through the vineyards, and that made it more enjoyable. Our friends would come out and they'd ride it with us."

In 1992, when the family moved to Aquebogue, Salim left to attend the University of California, Berkeley, where he studied nuclear engineering. "At the time, I was very much into the sciences and engineering and new technologies, stuff like that," he says. "Now I've kind of swung the other way."

During his college years Salim wasn't much interested in the winery, but that changed. "After 1996, when I graduated, that's when I came back home and saw what we had here. I realized it was a great opportunity and decided to become more involved."

When a guest asks just what it was that drew him back, Salim ponders a moment, then answers: "I guess the whole lifestyle. Just by being part of the family I get the opportunity to meet all types of people both in and out of the industry, not to mention all the people I meet here in the tasting room. So from that side I get to meet a whole cross section of people, which is very interesting. And then the opportunity to work with your hands, helping Nabeel with maintenance, and in the winery helping Kareem with things like washing tanks and cleaning hoses, pumping from one tank to another, topping barrels, all those types of things. They're not very cerebral, but they're the type of thing, at least for me, that once I finish them, I feel good. It's a rewarding activity."

Kareem begins to relate his story: "Even though I was eleven when my parents started the vineyard, I was young enough that I was still growing up with it, but old enough that I can remember the very

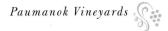

beginning. I remember my parents coming out and visiting the Hargraves after they read about them in the *New York Times,* traveling around the tristate area looking for farms, and finally closing on this one.

"In the 1980s we were just grape-growers, so we spent all of our time in the vineyard. It wasn't until 1990 that we renovated what used to be an old barn and built the winery, and we started making wine that year. So I grew up watching my parents grow the whole thing, and it was exciting. It was exciting to watch it happen and be part of it.

"I told my parents what I wanted to do upon graduation was to join them. I think they were a little bit shocked. You know, 'That's not why we're putting you through an Ivy League college.' They were like, 'Get a job.'

"So I did. I did end up working for two years in New York City for a small investment firm, but I decided I wasn't prepared to spend the rest of my life doing that. At the time I quit, I didn't necessarily intend to get right back into the wine business; I actually had all kinds of ideas of what I might do, but certainly coming back to the family winery was always on my list."

Kareem came back to work at Paumanok in the summer of 1998, helping out in the tasting room and working the harvest. "The only difference was, I had nowhere to go back to now," he says. "So what started off as a temporary arrangement, living and working here, turned into years. I went from literally doing a little bit of everything, which I still do—at one point I was more or less our sales rep for New York City—to basically making the wine with Charles and doing a lot of sales and marketing. I'm still in the vineyard when I can be, but not as much as I was a few years ago.

"I've done almost every aspect of the business,

Kareem Massoud

just like my parents have," Kareem says, "just like we all do in my family. We all pitch in wherever and whenever needed."

Though they all acknowledge how hard they work, the Massouds share a sense of accomplishment they say makes it all worthwhile.

Comparing the pressures of life on the vineyard to those of his corporate career, Charles says, "The magnitude of stress is very high, because we're dealing with Mother Nature and we have zero control over that. It runs our life, so to speak, the weather. And yet what you can do is very tangible, because you see where you started in the morning, and you can see and measure where you are at the end of the day, and you can say, 'OK, this is what I have contributed.' So I think in that sense it's a more healthy stress, even though it's not a smaller level of stress."

As for Kareem, he's fully committed to his choice of career. "I have absolutely no regrets. It's

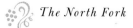

incredibly rewarding to do what we do. A lot of people—understandably so—have a somewhat naïve, romantic perception of what we do. You just watch the grapes grow and then go out and pick them when they're ripe, and presto! you have wine, and there's not a lot of work. It's an insane amount of work, the way we do it as an estate winery, from planting the vineyards all the way through bottling the wine and delivering it.

"But it's all worth it when you have a great vintage and you have great customers who appreciate what you do and who respect you and admire you for what you do. It's worth it all just for that," Kareem concludes.

In the end Charles are Ursula were very glad their three sons decided to join them in the family business. "Now that Ursula and I are slowing down a bit," says Charles, "it's a privilege to find out that we can actually continue to enjoy, through the children, what we started, which feels like yesterday, but we're talking over twenty-five years ago. For us it's a great story because it's been a succession of mostly wonderful things. We continue to this day to see it grow and blossom, and we enjoy every moment of it."

The Wines

Not knowing what would grow best on their land, the Massouds initially planted the grapes that made their favorite wines: Riesling, Chardonnay, Sauvignon Blanc, and Merlot. Later, they planted Cabernet Sauvignon and Cabernet Franc, and now they are gradually adding more varieties. All of them are doing so well, Charles says, that if he wanted to concentrate on fewer varieties, he wouldn't know what to pull out.

Paumanok's wine list is heavy with critically acclaimed wines. The vineyard's distance from the water allows it to stay warmer later into the season than areas farther east, where the peninsula is narrower and sea breezes cool the land; thus Cabernet Sauvignon, which needs a lot of sun and heat to ripen, can get fully ripe here, resulting in some of the top-rated wines of this varietal in New York State. Paumanok's premium red blend, Assemblage, has won the highest praise, and its Grand Vintage bottlings of Merlot and Cabernet Sauvignon are consistently well received by critics and customers.

Other wines currently offered include Festival Red table wine, Cabernet Franc, Merlot, Barrel-Fermented Chardonnay, Chenin Blanc, Riesling, Semi-Dry Riesling, and Late-Harvest Sauvignon Blanc.

Paumanok Vineyards
1074 Main Road, Aquebogue
(631) 722-8800
info@paumanok.com
www.paumanok.com
Open year-round
Owners: Charles and Ursula Massoud
Winemaker: Kareem Massoud
Founded: 1983
Acres planted: 72
Varieties grown: Chardonnay, Chenin Blanc, Riesling, Sauvignon Blanc, Cabernet Franc, Cabernet Sauvignon, Merlot, Petit Verdot
Long Island Wine Council member

JAMESPORT VINEYARDS

S ET BACK FROM THE MAIN ROAD IN JAMESPORT, A FORMER POTATO BARN HOUSES JAMESPORT VINEYARDS' WINERY AND TASTING ROOM. Acquired by Ron Goerler Sr. in 1986, the barn was converted to its current use and opened in 1989. Entering the foyer, visitors can see into the glass-walled lab, which also houses huge oak and stainless-steel tanks. The oak tanks look like giant wine barrels standing on end, and the effect is disorienting, as if you've suddenly shrunk, like Alice in Wonderland.

On the next level is a tasting room that retains the nostalgic ambience of a working barn. Wine barrels fitted with glass tabletops overlook the tank room and French doors reveal a lawn set into the vineyard, where umbrella-shaded tables invite lingering on a summer day.

Co-owner, Ron Goerler Jr.

It's easy to guess on first meeting Ron Goerler Jr. that he spends most of his time outdoors. He has that look of rugged, ruddy good health that defines a farmer, along with a love for the land that comes through strong and clear. Since the age of eighteen, he's been working in the family's vineyards; now he's the one in charge.

Ron's father and partner is Ron Sr. A harness driver in his younger days, he keeps the last of his horses at Early Rising Farm in Cutchogue, which he bought in 1981. Father and son live within a stone's throw of one another on the farm.

Ron Sr. owns a plumbing supply business. Ron Jr. worked there for a while, until he realized he wasn't cut out for an indoor job.

Ron Goerler Jr.

"I give my dad credit," Ron Jr. says. "He had the vision. I wouldn't be here if he hadn't taken the steps and wanted to be part of this industry.

"Any time you start a business," he continues, "it takes lots of guts, lots of money, and, most of all, passion and perseverance. To me the passion is watching the vineyard start from scratch. Looking at a piece of land, figuring out what goes on it—what root stock, what clone, what's the wine going to be like when it gets to a certain point—and then having all those things take place."

Like every farmer, Ron Jr. keeps a vigilant eye on the weather, which can be friend or enemy, or even change from one to the other in an instant.

"A hurricane could rip through this whole area in the middle of harvest," he says, "and guess what? That's life!" Recalling a tornado that hit the North Fork several years ago, Ron Jr. recounts, "It came through Jamesport, right through our place, wiped out our Syrah and moved out into the bay.

"You're dealing with Mother Nature, and regardless of what you think you know and how you want to do something, you have to change. The weather says no, you can't do that, you have to do it like this. In a wet year you can't push things. You get boxed into an area where you have to deal with

things fast, because otherwise the fruit's ruined."

Rough weather or calm, keeping up with his endless responsibilities isn't easy. "It's a challenge, running a vineyard—family in the middle—and then running a winery," Ron Jr. admits. "Just this morning I was talking to Richie Pisacano," he says, speaking of the owner of Roanoke Vineyards, "and he said, 'You've got five farms across the North Fork, a wife who works full time; you've got the kids and the business—how do you do it?' But that's the exciting part; that's the fun part. Does it get tiresome? Yes, it gets tiresome, but at the end of the day I know I've put my best effort into every bottle of wine I produce. That's the passion of it, when the customers say, 'Wow, this is really good wine!'"

Things have changed since he was thirteen. "I looked at my dad coming out here in 1981 and I thought, 'What the heck are we doing out here?' Now I wouldn't go anywhere else," he says. "I think what also drives me is the beauty this place has to offer. There are not too many unique places like the East End of Long Island. You've got the water, the farms, the fresh food, the wine. It takes a lot for all those things to jibe. You go to other areas, and they might have the beautiful waterfront; they might have the beautiful pastoral farms, or the mountains, or whatever it is, but to get all those things—when you think about it, it's a big deal."

That big deal is a big part of what makes Ron Jr. climb into the cab of his tractor day after day. And now that his son, Alex, is learning how to tend the vines, Ron harbors the hope that Jamesport Vineyards will one day pass into the hands of the third generation.

The Winemaker, Leslie Howard

Les Howard is a rarity: a homegrown winemaker with roots sunk deeply into the East End's fertile soil. "I grew up in New Suffolk," he says, referring to a small hamlet on Peconic Bay. "My ancestors, the Wells and Terry families, were farmers for generations."

Les began his career in the cellar of a Peconic winery. "I started working when I was nineteen, and then I got the idea I was going to be a winemaker. It sounded like fun, and I got very involved in it."

Taking increasingly responsible jobs at various East End wineries, he worked his way up to assistant winemaker, then was hired by Jamesport Vineyards in 2005. It's a good match.

"Ron's philosophy in the vineyard is exactly what I agree with," Les says. "When we pick the grapes at just the right time and they've been tended just the right way, you can really make some excellent wine."

When it comes to winemaking, Les thinks his broad experience gives him an advantage. "I was able to see different winemaking styles, work with different people. Then I brought all these styles together to create my own style."

Les describes the components that go into a blend as colors on a painter's palette. He and Ron Jr. get so caught up in the process that they have a hard time stopping. "Every time you try again," says Les, "you find, 'Oh, I like this one better than the last one.' You can get carried away," he admits with a smile.

The Wines

Jamesport Vineyards' wines are known for their ripe fruit and relatively low alcohol levels, making them pair especially well with food. Nearly every wine currently available has earned at least one medal, and two vintages of Cabernet Franc have been named Best Red Wine at the New York Wine and Food Classic.

Whites include part steel-fermented, part oak-fermented Sauvignon Blanc, East End Chardonnay, and Reserve Chardonnay. Reds include Merlot

Estate, Reserve Merlot, East End Merlot, Cabernet Franc, Pinot Noir, and Melange de Trois, the winery's signature blend of Cabernet Sauvignon, Merlot, and Cabernet Franc. Rounding out the current wine list is East End Rosé.

Jamesport Vineyards
1216 Main Road, Jamesport
(631) 722-5256
info@jamesport-vineyards.com
www.jamesport-vineyards.com
Open year-round
Owners: Ron Goerler Sr. and Ron Goerler Jr.
Winemaker: Les Howard
Founded: 1981
Acres planted: 60
Varieties grown: Chardonnay, Pinot Blanc,
Riesling, Sauvignon Blanc, Semillon,
Cabernet Franc, Cabernet Sauvignon,
Malbec, Merlot, Pinot Noir
Long Island Wine Council member

DILIBERTO WINERY

ILIBERTO WINERY'S TASTING ROOM IS HIDDEN FROM VIEW UNTIL YOU'RE NEARLY WITHIN REACH OF THE DOOR OF THE HANDSOME CEDAR-shingled structure. The first thing you notice is the pleasantly shaded wraparound porch, but the real surprise lies inside. The entire back wall of the tasting room is painted to resemble an Italian piazza, complete with a sign saying RISTORANTE BENEVENTO in honor of owner Salvatore Diliberto's mother, who came from the province of Benevento in the Campania region of Italy.

There's no stand-up tasting bar here; guests are invited to sit at small tables while they taste the wine, and Sal makes the rounds, personally greeting people with his special brand of Italian hospitality while his wife, Maryann, pours. A large-screen plasma TV might be showing mesmerizing aerial views of Italy, and the Three Tenors might be heard in the background. That's particularly appropriate, since Sal possesses a trained operatic voice and has been known to burst into exuberant song.

The Owners, Salvatore and Maryann Diliberto
Sal Diliberto is the kind of outgoing, friendly man who makes you feel like the two of you are old

friends the first time you meet. His love for what he's doing is evident in his voice, his broad smile, and every gesture. Maryann, though quieter than Sal, is every bit as welcoming. The Dilibertos go out of their way to make visitors to their tasting room feel like honored guests.

While wine was part of Sal's Italian heritage, it wasn't served with everyday meals in his childhood home in Queens; it was reserved for Sunday dinners and special occasions. He'd never seen anyone in his family make wine, but inspiration hit when he read about a man selling winemaking equipment out of his home. Sal bought a small crusher and press and a book called *Grapes into Wine.* His first grapes came from California, and he made the wine in five-gallon glass jars.

"We enjoyed the wine, and I enjoyed the process," Sal says. He turns to his wife. "And we love the smell, right, Maryann? We love the smell of fermenting grapes."

Nodding and laughing, Maryann responds, "Yes, but the fruit flies!"

"The fruit flies! Six billion fruit flies!" Sal laughs, then continues. "That's how it started. Once you do that, you kind of get hooked. We started making it every year, using California grapes, buying them at the terminal market in Brooklyn."

A turning point came when the Dilibertos were visiting a cousin of Maryann who was renting a house on the North Fork. "I passed by Peconic Bay Vineyard, and I saw the phone number on the sign and called it when I got back home," Sal remembers. For the next ten years, he bought grapes from Ray Blum, one of the East End's pioneering vintners.

"I really got to enjoy coming out here, being here at harvest time, picking up the grapes and seeing what was going on," Sal says. "We started to look for little piece of property and found this in '91."

In 1997 the Dilibertos converted a barn on their property into a spacious home. They planted their

Maryann and Sal Diliberto

first vines in 1998 and produced their first wines in 2001. If he was dismayed when he realized the hard work he was in for, Sal doesn't show it. "If you want to grow your own grapes," he says, "you have to contend with all the problems farmers have to contend with. It's a year-by-year learning experience—hailstorms, Japanese beetles, grape berry moths, continuous rain for nine days at the end of the growing season ... so many different things that farmers have absolutely no control over."

The vagaries of growing a crop have given him a great respect for farmers. "I've told them how much I appreciate what they've had to go through all these years," he says, "and one farmer used to say, 'Yeah, you gotta go through a lot, but in the end, you're still out here.' I can relate to that. And it's a good feeling

at the end of the season, seeing that you've got the grapes to come in healthy and in the quantity you hoped to get."

Sal tells a story about the property next door to his, which he discovered was owned by a man also named Sal who lived five minutes from him in Queens. When Sal asked the other Sal why he bought land in Jamesport, he answered in a thick Italian accent, "Well, you know, when I see this land, it remind me of Sicily."

"I told him I'd never been to Sicily," Sal recounts, "but maybe there's something out here on the North Fork, something in my blood, that makes me think of Sicily."

Though as of this writing Sal still spends part of the week at his elder-law practice in Queens and

Maryann, who has completed a sommelier's course, works as a substitute teacher in Riverhead, both are fully committed to the ongoing success of their commercial wine venture.

"I'm in awe of Sal," says Maryann. "He's living his dream." Her husband responds with a hearty laugh, "Yeah, there's nothing like dreaming about hard work!"

The Wines

The Dilibertos produce only a thousand cases a year and don't plan to get much bigger than that. "Everything we do is done on a small scale, and to some extent I think that's probably the best part of our operation," Sal declares. Working with small batches keeps the fermenting juice cooler, and he believes that lends a softness to his wines. "Our strength is in being able to make wines that I think are softer. And we don't have to rush to bring things to the market.

"I have a little separation anxiety when it comes to selling my wine," he adds. "We never rushed to sell it, so we've been accumulating the wine. We have '01, '02, '03, and '04, and I'd like to think we can continue doing the same thing: not rushing to get a wine out there." He won't let a vintage go into the tasting room until he feels it's ready to be drunk, so if someone asks him when they should open a particular bottle, Sal responds, "What time is dinner?"

Tasting flights rotate on an eight-week schedule, running through several vintages of Burgundy-style Chardonnay; Merlot; Cabernet Sauvignon; Cabernet Franc; a half-Merlot, half–Cabernet Franc Chianti-style blend called Cantina; and Tre, a Bordeaux blend.

In the Dilibertos' debut wine competition, the 2004 New York Wine and Food Classic, all three wines submitted—2001 Merlot, 2002 Merlot, and 2001 Tre—earned gold medals. In the 2005 Classic the 2003 Merlot was named Best Merlot. And in the 2007 Classic both the 2001 Cabernet Sauvignon and 2004 Cantina walked away with silver.

Diliberto Winery
250 Manor Lane, Jamesport
(631) 722-3416
diliberto1@msn.com
www.dilibertowinery.com
Open year-round
Owners: Salvatore and Maryann Diliberto
Winemaker: Salvatore Diliberto
Founded: 1998
Acres planted: 4
Varieties grown: Chardonnay, Cabernet Franc, Cabernet Sauvignon, Merlot
Long Island Wine Council member

CLOVIS POINT

O<small>N THE MAIN ROAD, NEAR THE CENTER OF THE HAMLET OF JAMESPORT, IS A HANDSOME RED SIGN ANNOUNCING THE LOCATION OF</small> Clovis Point. The name is taken from sculpted stone spear tips believed to have been used by the area's inhabitants some ten thousand years ago.

A landscaped walkway leads to mahogany-framed doors in the end wall of a converted 1920s potato barn. The vineyard is to your left, but the full effect of the view can't be experienced until you go through the tasting room onto the balustraded patio. There your eyes are drawn to the vineyard by a wide swath of manicured lawn. Beyond the vines, verdant farm fields flow unbroken to a dense line of trees. Not a single manmade structure is in sight. It's a rare and peaceful vista, one worth savoring over a glass of wine under one of the patio's big red umbrellas.

Clovis Point's tasting room has been carefully renovated, leaving the old barn's structure intact. Cedar shakes and vertical barn wood cover the exterior, while slatelike shingles and a charming cupola, complete with weathervane, adorn the copper-edged roof. Rich mahogany outlines the glass-paneled doors and windows. Inside, the tasting

Hal Ginsburg and Nasrallah Misk

room, with its bluestone floor, extends the full length of the building and the long, elegant bar offers plenty of elbow room.

The Managing Partners, Nasrallah Misk and Hal Ginsburg

At first glance Hal Ginsburg and Nasrallah Misk would seem to have little in common. They're of different generations; Hal is from New York while Nasrallah, who goes by Misk, is originally from Lebanon; Hal is an attorney and Misk is a real estate developer. But their similarities outweigh their differences. Both live and work in Queens, both love wine and the North Fork, and they share a passion for making "a good bottle of wine."

Hal and Misk—who founded Clovis Point with Mary Bayno, John and Renae Pine, and Richard Frey—have a family connection through Hal's business partner, who is Misk's son. They've been good friends for more than twenty-five years.

"Our business lives intertwined," Misk says. "It's like a family business. I call Hal my number five son."

The two began visiting the North Fork in the mid-1970s and enjoyed watching the progress of the fledgling wine industry. Around the same time each of them bought a second home here, in 2000, they decided to turn their growing dream of starting a winery into a reality.

"We were both at points in our lives when we wanted a new project," says Misk, "and this seemed like something we would love to do. So we said, 'Why not a vineyard?' Our involvement is out of passion. We both love red wine. We only want to make a good bottle of wine."

Some of Hal's passion was sparked by an earlier experience. "I got married at a college friend's vineyard in Oregon," he says. "He'd built the vineyard from scratch, and I found that inspiring."

The two assembled a group of partners, and in 2001 they bought ten acres of farmland. In 2002 they added an existing vineyard that holds some of the oldest vines on the North Fork.

"We spare no expense to bring in good wine," Misk says, and Hal adds with a wry smile, "Now if we could just learn how to control the weather."

On a hot summer day, over the remnants of a delicious alfresco lunch on the patio, Misk tries to explain to a guest why the love of wine transcends the pleasures of the senses.

mostly in stainless steel with a little barrel-fermented Chardonnay and some Gewürztraminer added. The steel-fermented 2004 Chardonnay was awarded a silver medal in the 2007 International Eastern Wine Competition. As of this writing, that wine and the 2005 Barrel-Fermented Chardonnay are available.

Also currently in the tasting room are the 2004 Merlot, 2004 Vintner's Select Merlot, and 2005 Cabernet Franc. Vintner's Select wines are made only in the best vintage years. The 2004 Merlot is blended with Cabernet Franc and small amounts of Cabernet Sauvignon and Petit Verdot. The 2004 Vintner's Select is 89 percent Merlot, with roughly equal amounts of Petit Verdot, Malbec, and Cabernet Sauvignon.

Artifact, a new release as this is written, is a Bordeaux-style red blend of 88 percent Merlot, 6 percent Cabernet Sauvignon, and 6 percent Cabernet Franc.

"Enjoying wine is also psychological," he says, "and for me, it's also something in history."

Then, with a contented grin, he raises a ruby glass of Clovis Point 2004 Vintner's Select Merlot in a silent toast to the many delights of fine wine.

The Wines

The aim of winemaking at Clovis Point is to create the best possible varietal blends. "It's not important to us to say '100 percent,'" says Hal. "We're focused on making the best wine we can," concurs Misk. "'One hundred percent estate' doesn't mean the grapes are any good."

The partners hired the highly experienced John Leo of Premium Wine Group, the North Fork's one and only custom-crush facility, to shepherd their wines from vine to bottle. They trust their winemaker implicitly and extend him the freedom he needs to bring out the best potential of the fruit, resulting in balanced, elegant wines that unfold in the mouth in a most gratifying way.

Clovis Point's initial bottlings, which brought home several medals, were limited to Merlot and Chardonnay. The winery has since branched out to include Cabernet Franc and Cabernet Sauvignon.

Chardonnay is currently produced in two styles, one aged in French oak and the other fermented

Clovis Point
1935 Main Road, Jamesport
(631) 722-4222
info@clovispointwines.com
www.clovispointwines.com
Open year-round
Owners: Nasrallah Misk, Hal Ginsburg,
Mary Bayno, John and Renae Pine, and
Richard Frey
Winemaker: John Leo
Founded: 2001
Acres planted: 20
Varieties grown: Chardonnay, Cabernet
Franc, Merlot, Syrah
Long Island Wine Council member

HANDMADE RICOTTA GNOCCHI WITH NORTH FORK FARM STAND VEGETABLE BASIL BROTH AND REGGIANO

Jedediah Hawkins Inn, Jamesport | *Michael Ross and Tom Schaudel, chefs*

Gnocchi
- 1 pound ricotta cheese, drained
- 1 cup flour
- 1 whole egg
- 1 tablespoon truffle oil (optional)
- Salt and pepper to taste

Sauce
- 2 tablespoons olive oil
- Assorted farm stand vegetables:
  - Peas, shelled
  - Corn, cut from ear
  - Zucchini, diced
  - Summer squash, diced
  - Cherry tomatoes, halved
  - Favas, shelled
  - Other seasonal vegetables, as desired
- ½ cup basil pesto
- ½ cup chicken or vegetable stock
- Shaved Reggiano

1. Mix all gnocchi ingredients together and form a ball. Wrap in plastic wrap and refrigerate for 3 hours.
2. On a floured surface, roll chilled dough into a rope about ¾-inch thick; cut into 1-inch pieces. Bring a pot of salted water to a boil. Drop in gnocchi. When gnocchi float to the top, remove with a slotted spoon and place in ice water.
3. When gnocchi are cool, drain and coat them in oil. Store gnocchi in the refrigerator and reheat when needed.
4. For the sauce, heat olive oil in a sauté pan. Add vegetables and cook until just tender. Add pesto and stock. Heat well, stirring to combine.
5. Reheat gnocchi and toss with vegetables. Transfer to a serving bowl and top with shaved Reggiano.

Serves 6–10, depending on the amount of vegetables used. Pair with a Long Island Sauvignon Blanc.

LAUREL LAKE VINEYARDS

ITH ITS FOUR DORMERS, TWIN GABLE-END CHIMNEYS, AND BALUSTRADED VERANDA, LAUREL LAKE VINEYARDS' TASTING ROOM is a pleasing combination of Colonial and Southern Ranch architecture. The veranda opens onto a deck overlooking the vineyard. The spacious tasting room has an antique bar, stained-glass windows, bistro tables for indoor sipping, and a gift shop.

Chardonnay vines were planted here in 1980, making them among the oldest on the East End. In 1999 a group of Chilean winemakers bought the business. Since then they have brought in new winemaking equipment, expanded their acreage, and planted additional varieties, including Sauvignon Blanc, Merlot, Shiraz (Syrah), and Sangiovese.

Co-owner and Winemaker, Juan Esteban Sepulveda

Juan Esteban Sepulveda co-owns Laurel Lake with two impressive partners. Alejandro Parot owns a winery in Chile that sells millions of gallons annually. He is renowned as one of the greatest enologists in the industry and holds a permanent judge's seat at the world's most prestigious wine competition, held each year in Brussels. Francisco Gillmore also owns a very large vineyard and winery in Chile.

Juan lives on the North Fork and works full-time at Laurel Lake. On a clear, crisp January day, he escorts a visitor on a tasting tour of the winery while they talk about his background, how a group of Chilean winemakers found their way to the

North Fork, and what's going on at Laurel Lake Vineyards.

Juan's charming accent and sentence structure retain the imprint of his native Chile.

"I come from a family of grape-growers and winemakers," he begins. "I grew up on the farm helping my father plant vineyards, harvesting the grapes, and I work with an uncle making wine for many years. For some reason—I was young—I decided to be an economist, not a winemaker."

The story Juan tells then is one that can be heard from several young Long Island winemakers: They leave the vineyard life behind for the world of business, but soon find that the lure of the vines is stronger than they thought.

"I have a marketing degree," Juan continues, "and I started working in business—entrepreneur, stock market—but after a year and a half, that's enough for me. I finished my studies in Japan and went back to Chile. It's a lot of fun, but I have more fun in the wine business."

Back in Chile, Juan worked for companies connected with his family's business. He traveled to many other wine regions, encouraging big wine companies to come to Chile. "That way, our eyes are not focused only on Chilean wine, and we decided to invest outside the country," he says.

It was on one of his trips that Juan more or less stumbled across the Long Island wine region. Stuck in New York City for three days between flights, he took the suggestion of a winemaker friend and visited the North Fork.

"I said, 'What's there besides the beach and besides the Hamptons?' I didn't know what else. He said, 'There are a few wineries over there and you might enjoy it, because in the summer it's very nice.' And I came over here and said, 'It's beautiful!' It's

one hour and a half from Manhattan, it's a beautiful place to live, it's quiet, it's next to the beach, people are more friendly, and the food is great, the vegetables are great. It's right in the corner; I don't have to be in upstate New York, where it's far away from everything, and it's a very cold winter over there. And I said, 'This is great!' I tasted some of the wine, and there are good wines and I can see the potential."

He returned to Chile excited about his discovery, and the future partners started searching for North Fork property. "We were ready to buy a piece of land," Juan says, "and for some reason we couldn't close it, and Laurel Lake appeared and we decided to buy Laurel Lake instead of that land. Because I was involved in all this processing, I became a partner and I decided to move over here."

After several years here Juan and his wife, Juana, moved back to Chile. They returned in 2007 to continue raising their three children on the North Fork.

Juan is still in love with the North Fork and all it has to offer. "I used to live in Santiago, the capital of Chile. And wherever you go, those cities are too big. The people run over the other people, because always they're late for something. In the country you have the time, you take your time to do all the jobs. You do the same work over here as there, with a more relaxing, better quality of life."

The Wines
Juan leads his guest through a room where gleaming stainless-steel tanks rise nearly to the ceiling.

"This is our fermenting room, where we make all the wine," he says. "We have two levels of wine. We have what we call Estate, fermented in stainless steel—very light, crisp flavor, pure Long Island

flavor. When you drink wine, you get a combination of flavors. But what we're trying to do over here is enlarge and encapsulate Long Island flavor—pure. In that way we have distinguished it from any other country."

Passing into the barrel room, Juan says, "Over here we ferment and store our Reserve wine. Our future is here, because we have wine for our future use. Our opportunity is right in this place."

He extracts two samples of Chardonnay from a barrel with a large glass tube called a wine thief, and Juan and his guest both taste—swirling, sniffing deeply, drawing the wine over the tongue, letting it fill all the corners of the mouth, then spitting the golden liquid into a bucket. While his guest tastes again and ponders the nuances of the wine, Juan talks about the differences between Long Island and Chilean wines.

"In the long term, here on Long Island we can produce outstanding and very elegant, complex wine, red and white. That way we can have more oak, French oak, and combine that flavor with the elegant flavor of Long Island," Juan explains.

"With the aging—Long Island is very good for aging—we can make an outstanding wine," he continues. "This is a Chardonnay 2005, and if you compare it to a wine from a warm-weather country, it is different. Those wines age very quickly, but over here, because we have a strong acidity in the wine, the wine lasts longer. The fresh flavor lasts a much longer time, and the aging of the oak gives it a very elegant flavor, more structure. It fills all the gaps in your mouth." His guest concurs: This is a lovely, well-structured, mouth-filling wine.

"You see," Juan responds with evident pleasure, "very nice, refreshing flavor. The wine is very dry, but the aging makes the wine much smoother and the oak adds a very nice complement.

"That goes very well with food," Juan is quick to add. "Long Island seafood—we have it right here. We can go to the beach and take it! It cannot be more fresh than that. That's perfect. In summertime we can get so much great food, seafood—that is a very nice combination."

Juan takes a sample from another barrel. As he lets the contents of the wine thief drain into the visitor's glass, he says, "Enjoy this barrel, because it is 2001. Yes, this is '01 Cabernet Sauvignon." He holds up his glass to show the sign of aging at the edges of the wine. "We can see in the color, this brick color all around, but just from the smell we can see the complexity of the wine. It's very attractive, no?

"You see, this is 2001; we're talking about seven years," Juan continues. "This is what Long Island can produce. Very nice wine—seven years. I think I have three or four barrels. I keep it for part of the history, to see how long we can age the wine, what's happening to the wine with the aging. But you see, I use now old barrels, because I think we have enough oak in the wine, and I like to keep the flavor of the grapes, the Long Island expression."

Unfortunately for Laurel Lake's customers, this wine is not for sale. "It's part library and part blending," Juan explains. "I like blended wine. For example, in our Reserve 2003, I put a little bit of 2001—5 percent, 7 percent. It depends on the final blend, the tasting at the moment. That way I keep some of the complexity of the old wine and the fresh flavor of the new wine, and make the new expression of a unique wine. But with this wine, we can see the projection that we can have with Long Island wine."

Returning to the difference between winemaking in his home country and on Long Island, Juan says,

"Over here we can grow very nice wine, different than Chile. That doesn't mean Chile cannot produce very good wine, or California cannot produce good wine, too. We can produce good wine almost everywhere in the world today. But over here for us is a challenge, because it's very different from Chile. First, in Chile we don't have snow in the valley; we have snow in the mountains. Working with winter is very challenging for us. There, our winter is 45, 48 degrees, the lowest temperature.

"Second, we don't have stores over there like over here," Juan says, referring to the tasting room, where wines are sold at retail. "This is something absolutely new for us, and it's very attractive, because in the end we make the wine not for ourselves, but to share with other people. In Chile, when we make the wine and ship to everywhere in the world, we never get to see the faces enjoying the wine. Over here we have the chance to talk, even to get the feedback in terms of if we're doing right or not. When we get this contact, we can make it even better—or at least we'll try. And that is something different.

"If you go, for instance, to countries like Chile

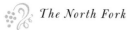

and Australia and New Zealand or South Africa," he says, "you will see vineyards that are far away from any city. You would take two hours to drive just to get to the winery, and another forty-five minutes to get to the following winery, and between those wineries, nothing.

"And we like people; we like to see people; we like to share the wine. Of course it's very hard work, tasting the wine all day long, working with the wine, and at the end of the day, drinking it yourself—it makes it much harder. If we can share that, it makes much more reward to our job."

White wines currently offered at Laurel Lake are the stainless-steel-fermented Chardonnay Estate, Chardonnay Estate Bottled Reserve, Riesling, Wind Song White, Moscato Sparkling, and Ice Wine. Two rosés are on the wine list at this writing: Lake Rosé and Wind Song Blush.

In reds the winery makes Wind Song Red, Merlot, Syrah, Cabernet Sauvignon, Cabernet

Sauvignon Reserve, Cabernet Franc, Pinot Noir, and Meritage, a small-production Bordeaux blend.

Laurel Lake Vineyards
3165 Main Road, Laurel
(631) 298-1420
info@llwines.com
www.llwines.com
Open year-round
Owners: Alejandro Parot, Francisco Gillmore, and Juan Esteban Sepulveda
Winemaker: Juan Esteban Sepulveda
Founded: 1980
Acres planted: 24
Varieties grown: Chardonnay, Sauvignon Blanc, Merlot, Shiraz/Syrah, Sangiovese
Long Island Wine Council member

HARBES FAMILY VINEYARD

No East End winemaking family has deeper roots in farming than Ed and Monica Harbes and their eight children: Ed's ancestors have been tilling Long Island soil since the 1600s. In 1968 his father moved the farming operation to Mattituck, and Ed and his new bride began plowing and planting ten years later.

Today they own a thriving business with farm stands and "agritainment" attractions in Mattituck and Jamesport and a pumpkin farm in Riverhead. The tasting room, a small barn near the Mattituck farm stand, charms visitors with its authentic rusticity.

The Owners, The Harbes family

To learn the story behind their vineyard venture, a guest sat with several members of the Harbes family at their massive dining room table on a chill and misty February morning. Beyond the bay window naked vines stood under a low, gray sky.

Monica Harbes (née Meyers/Baker) ended up on Long Island because of a terrible tragedy: Her parents, vegetable and dairy farmers in Minnesota, were killed in a car accident, leaving their nine children orphaned. Monica was adopted by a family in Charlotte, North Carolina, and later came to Long

family, I needed an industry that was more likely to increase.

"So we started with the corn and farm stand in 1989, and that's grown over the years. But I had a number of sons and daughters in college, and I believed if we had an attractive enough opportunity, they would perhaps decide to join us in the family business. Vegetable farming, as I mentioned, was on the decrease along with potatoes, and I thought perhaps our sons and daughters would be interested in the vineyard industry. We planted five acres on that speculation in 2003. We're going on our fifth season now and, even though it wasn't a sure thing at the time, my son Edward has taken a serious interest in the business. He's decided to manage our vineyard and is also beginning to make wine."

Asked if he was enthusiastic about the family's branching out into the wine business, Edward replies, "I definitely was. I recall, when I was growing up, starting to see the vineyards sprout up, and I always thought it would be really neat to have our own vineyard and be able to make our own wine. When I was going to college, my parents undertook a serious effort to learn about the business and research all the different things involved, including the selection of the site, which is probably the most important thing when you're planting a vineyard.

"I graduated [from Cornell College of Agriculture and Life Sciences] in 2005 and spent a year in New York City working in financial services, just enough to get my feet wet and kind of see what was out there, see what other businesses were like and what the corporate world was like, what it was like to live in Manhattan. It was definitely very nice, but after a year there I decided to come back here."

The first task Edward took on was organizing the office. "At the same time, I was learning more

Island to live with her sister. "On the first day in high school," Monica recalls, "I met my husband-to-be in art class, and in 1978 we got married. I married a farmer, so I guess it was kind of in my blood. I did go back to Minnesota where I was from and, interestingly enough, it looks similar to this area."

Ed Harbes—not to be confused with his son Edward Jr.—picks up the agricultural tale. "I initially started with my father in the wholesale potato industry. In the 1970s potatoes were still having a pretty good run. It was maybe, oh, twenty to thirty thousand acres of potatoes here at that point. Now I understand there's less than three thousand. I could see that potato farming was an industry that would likely continue to decrease and, since we had a large

about the vineyard and becoming more involved in the management. And the second year I was in charge of it entirely myself, and it went very well. I worked part-time with Chris Kelly, a local vineyard manager, just to get a sense of how managing a vineyard on the North Fork is different from other areas. I purchased a bunch of books—you know, you read about different parts of the world. Everyone has their own take and some things work better in different places, depending on the environment and what kind of weather you have, and the soils—*terroir* is the word they use to describe all that."

Edward continues, growing more animated. "Two thousand and seven was one of the bumper vintages, as everyone's aware. It was really exciting to pull in a big harvest after my first year. I didn't make too many mistakes, thankfully. And I also started making some of my own wine, some Merlot, this year. It's a fun experience. It's just a whole different world compared to traditional row-crop farming. In general the goal is to combine what the North Fork has to offer in a retail setting, where people can come experience the fruits, the vegetables, the wine, and just trying to bring that all under one roof. It's long and hard, but I think we'll get there."

Until they have their own winemaking facility, most of the wine is being made at Paumanok Vineyards under the supervision of Charles and Kareem Massoud. The Harbes tasting room is a small barn near the family's Mattituck farm stand. There are plans afoot to expand, improve, and perhaps move it, but probably not very far, they say.

The family works together on most projects, but everyone has a specialty. The popular corn maze at the Jamesport farm stand is designed every year by Edward's younger brothers, David and Daniel, with David taking the lead and Dan pitching in. Daughters

Sarah and Lisa, both still in high school, help mow the young corn into intricate patterns.

Following in the family footsteps, David is about to graduate from Cornell, and Dan has been accepted there.

"David's unique interest is retailing in general, both with the wine and the current farm market," Ed says. "He'd like to take our facilities to the next level, and I certainly welcome that interest. And my son Daniel has always been interested and involved with our business. He was my first maze sales representative. He was probably eight years old at the time, something like that, but did the job well. And he's been managing some of our farm stand locations over the years, Jamesport in particular."

Dan jumps in: "I'm considering taking some classes in viticulture at Cornell, so I might consider pursuing the vineyard as well. I'm not sure whether I'll actually do it or not, but it would be interesting."

Jason, the eldest son, founded the family's Mattituck farm stand at the tender age of ten. According to Sarah, her big brother Jay was wise beyond his years. "He'd always try to barter with the customers and stuff like that," she says with a smile.

Daughters Evelyn and Jessica are also involved in the family business, Evelyn assisting with marketing efforts and Jessica managing the retail end.

Sarah and Lisa are busy with schoolwork and helping out at the farm stands, but they pitch in at the vineyard when they can, doing a little pruning and picking up what Sarah calls "the sticks." Lisa wants to go to Cornell, but Sarah hasn't quite made up her mind yet.

The attention turns back to Monica with a question about her life in farming. She smiles and says, "Well, I have eight children, so I've given raising my children priority, of course. But then

again, secondly came helping my husband, whether it meant planting cabbage, cutting cabbage, cutting cauliflower, boxing cauliflower, grading potatoes, digging potatoes, driving the truck—you name it, I've done it. Just about everything, with kids in tow, usually. So it's really been an integral part of my life and continues to be.

"I was very excited about having a vineyard," Monica continues. "I thought it was a particular niche that one of our sons or maybe a couple of our kids could really take and run with, because I could see five years ago that that particular industry was making headway, whereas row-crop farming is kind of becoming a thing of the past almost, unfortunately.

"And of course I have a real heart for agriculture and the beauty of the land that we live in in this area, so I thought it would be important to do whatever I could to see it remain in agriculture. We have preserved a good portion of our land here, so you'll never see townhouses built on it, or homes, and you'll always hopefully see a beautiful vineyard, a well-maintained vineyard. So I thought that would be a nice direction to head into."

Some of those gathered around the table gaze out the window at the vineyard, still shrouded in mist, as Monica begins to relate how they chose this site. "This particular spot, we found by talking to Louisa Hargrave; when she and her husband were scouting out a piece of property to have a vineyard, this actually was one of their favorite spots."

It's a good site for a vineyard, she goes on to explain, because it has southern exposure and the soil contains a lot of gravel. "It's similar to France's *terroir*," Monica explains, "so we're pretty happy with it."

"We spent a couple of years doing research," Monica goes on. "Of course, Ed did the primary research, but I helped with what little bit I could, researching the different clones. That was really important. We only have a small amount that we're growing, so we had to make sure we'd get excellent-tasting fruit, which will transfer over into good wine, hopefully."

Returning to the table from a brief errand, Ed asks Monica if she mentioned their favorite crop. "The way I like to put it," he says, "is the favorite crop on our farm has been our children. That's the reason that we work a little harder and a little longer. We have more economic motivation, for one thing. We've put five children through college and we have three more to go, so if that doesn't keep you motivated, I don't know what will!"

Ed and Monica ultimately decided to use several different clones of Chardonnay and Merlot vines. "We did take a lot of pains to choose what I consider the best-tasting varieties," says Ed. "And what I've learned since is that the combination of different clones has a special synergistic effect. In other words, this, that, and the other clone combined have a unique synergy, a group of characteristics that you can't realistically expect out of any one clone."

As the conversation draws to a close, Monica tells a story, one that is obviously dear to her heart. "When our oldest son, Jason, got married in 2006," she begins, "he and his wife, Dana, put in a special request. They wanted to serve our wine, which was our first-yield harvest, at their wedding. So it kind of debuted, and to me it was very touching because my husband, when he gave the toast, mentioned that that was Jesus's first miracle, turning water into wine."

Ed elaborates: "It was something to the effect that, 'Jesus was able to turn water into wine at the wedding at Cana. Unfortunately, we have nowhere near that ability, so we had to do it the hard way.'"

The Wines
Harbes Family Vineyard releases at this writing include Reserve Chardonnay, Wooden Wheel Chardonnay, Yellow House Chardonnay, and Old Barn Merlot.

Harbes Family Vineyard
715 Sound Avenue, Mattituck
(631) 298-0800
harbes@harbesfamilyfarm.com
www.harbesfamilyfarm.com
Open May through October
Owners: The Harbes family
Winemaking team: Edward Harbes Jr. and Charles and Kareem Massoud
Founded: 2003
Acres planted: 5
Varieties grown: Chardonnay, Merlot
Long Island Wine Council member

MACARI VINEYARDS & WINERY

A LOW STONE WALL SURMOUNTED BY AN ARCHED SIGN AT THE CORNER OF SOUND AND BERGEN AVENUES MARKS THE ENTRANCE TO MACARI Vineyards & Winery. A curving gravel drive leads to the tasting room, a structure that combines traditional and modern for a European look that manages to blend in with its farm-country setting. Most striking is the open-beamed, wood-and-stainless-steel arch over the front deck, a shape that echoes the entrance sign and subtly ties it all together.

Indoors, the vaulted ceiling, massive stone fireplace, and long stainless-steel tasting bar make the light-filled room seem even larger than it is. A few bistro tables are arranged near the fireplace, whose mantel is lined with wine bottles draped in gold, silver, and bronze medals suspended from colorful ribbons. Two sets of glass doors flank the fireplace, inviting guests to venture onto the covered deck overlooking the vineyard.

The Macari family's estate encompasses the two-hundred-acre vineyard and a farm complete with cows, goats, ducks, and donkeys. Its rolling hills and hollows gently undulate all the way to the sandy bluffs overlooking Long Island Sound.

After purchasing an existing vineyard and winery in 1994, the Macari family set about refurbishing and expanding both. The redesigned and remodeled tasting room opened its doors in 1998. Macari Vineyards has a second tasting room, Macari 2, on the Main Road in Cutchogue.

The Owners, the Macari Family

Joseph Macari Sr. and his daughter-in-law, Alexandra Macari, sit down with a visitor on a quiet March morning to talk about the family business. Joe Jr., who manages the vines, has pressing matters to attend to.

Asked when he first thought about starting a vineyard and winery, Joseph responds, "I think we started with the farm first. We just decided to plant some grapes, and it grew like a mushroom."

Not long after the Hargraves planted the first Long Island vineyard in 1973, Joseph hired vineyard expert Dave Mudd to advise him about planting his own vines. "I had a plan made up for a winery, for growing grapes, plus some housing around the fields out there," he says. "But somehow we never got off the ground with that."

"It was twenty-two or twenty-four years later when it did happen, because I found that booklet," Alexandra says. "So it's kind of interesting that the concept was there."

"Basically we were so busy in Queens and New York that we had no time to get back out here," her father-in-law explains. "We summered out here every year; that is, the family did. I would come out weekends. We shelved the idea until Joe and Alex moved to Cutchogue, and then we decided to start planting some grapes."

Their plan was to convert a barn on their farm to a winery, but then Mattituck Hills Winery came on the market and they purchased it instead. "From that time the wine industry has changed tremendously, with more and more people here," Joseph says. "It's become a tourist destination far greater than we ever imagined."

Alexandra recounts their beginnings: "When we first started, I remember Bob Henn and Wojtek Majewski—they were the first people that worked with us. The office was the kitchen table at home, and they started with learning how to plant. We didn't know anything then. Joe came with a laser

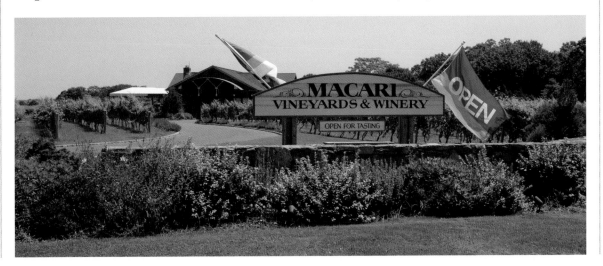

planter from Germany, and everyone was like, 'Sure, they know what they're doing!' There was an article in the *Suffolk Times,* 'They're thinking too big.' And then, after that, everyone had to come and see what this laser planter could do, and everyone criticized it. But now the funny thing is, people have purchased that machine, even purchased our own machine to do that style of planting. You know, try to follow a row, a straight string! We see the changes in technology, which is pretty amazing."

Before moving to the North Fork, Alexandra and Joe lived in Queens, where Joe worked in the family's real estate business, a concern that's still going strong after sixty years.

"Joe and Alex are basically the ones who run this winery," asserts Joseph Sr. "They know what's going on. They're here ninety hours a day."

Alexandra laughs. "We're not allowed to say it's a black hole anymore," she declares with rueful good humor. "I went to a seminar. We're supposed to be nice; it's supposed to be the white hole!

"But you know," she continues, "even the kids help during the season. You need help, you have to call them." Then, with a mischievous smile, she adds, "We call Grandpa first!"

Joe strides quickly through the tasting room, giving a sketchy wave as he rushes to fulfill another of his endless tasks.

"Joe does the vineyard managing, also," Alexandra says, "so we don't have another vineyard manager on staff. We're kind of an unusual team here: two flying winemakers [consultants who work for multiple wineries, often on different continents] and Joe doing outside. Joe has this whole program that he does outside, you know, with the fish and the horns and all that."

Alexandra is talking about organic farming and a system called biodynamics, which uses the positions of the moon and stars and other natural signs to guide agricultural practices.

"Everyone's going green now; it's the big thing," Alexandra says. "It's just better for our region. We had bees here, and they died because the other vineyards were spraying. You affect everyone surrounding you when you do something like that. But I guess Joe started farming organically ten years ago. Again, people thought we were kooky. He knew it worked; the soil improvements definitely show in the quality of the wine."

Some of those soil improvements include ground fish heads and composted manure from their small herd of Texas longhorn and Hereford cattle.

When her guest asks about the theory behind biodynamics, Alexandra responds, "You have to read the good old books of Rudolph Kiner, which are very complicated to read, but Joe reads those and he believes in it. We had Alan York working with us from California for three years, four years. He's the guru of biodynamics. It's quite interesting. You feed the life force, and that's the important thing," she says.

Feeding the life force can be thought of in another way, and Alexandra expresses it a little later, when the discussion turns to the subject of gold medals, high scores, and the individuality of taste.

"It's all about your taste buds," she says. "I always say—in French it's *chacun à son gout.*"

"Each to his taste," her guest responds.

"Yes, and it's so perfectly said, because not everyone enjoys the same thing. So get the bottle out, sit down, and have a glass! That's what it's about, you know. And of course we always think about food with it, in this place, especially. It's the most enjoyable way."

The Winemakers, Paola Valverde and Helmut Gangl

"Flying winemakers" Helmut Gangl and Paola Valverde lend Macari Vineyards an international flair. Helmut is from Austria and Paola is from Chile; both have an interesting story to tell about how they came to ply their trade on the East End of Long Island.

Paola, an engaging young woman with a shy smile, speaks with the strong inflections of her native country as she describes the journey that led her to the North Fork.

In Chile, she explains, students of agriculture must first study agronomy engineering. "Then you decide which area you want," she says. "One summer when I was a student, the owner of a winery in Chile said if I want to work with him I can go there and work for the summertime." It was the first time she had ever been inside a winery; she liked it so much she decided to complete her studies in winemaking.

Paola had just finished working for the international wine company Miguel Torres when she decided to try to find work in the United States. "Always I liked the wine from here," Paola explains, "and so I say I will try something different, because my country is very warm, and I want to try a different climate, like a cold climate."

She looked for an exchange program on the Internet. Macari Vineyards was seeking an assistant winemaker through such a program, so in 2003 Paola came to assist Helmut, who was Macari's solo winemaker at that time. Not long after, Paola was hired as co-winemaker.

Helmut's story begins on the other side of the world, in his native Austria. "I grew up with the wine since I was a little child," he recalls. "My father is a winegrower, and so I have to go and work with him every day, so yes, I grew up with the wine. I studied at the University of Agriculture in Vienna, and there I studied wine production, vinification and so on."

Beginning in 1991, Helmut worked for the Austrian government's Official Institution in Eisenstadt, searching the vines for viruses and other diseases and the cellar for yeasts. "But what I prefer at home," he says, "is our little vineyard, our little winery. There we make sweet wines because our climate, our soil, our weather is very, very good for this."

Helmut met Joe Macari Jr. at an international wine fair in New York City's Soho district in 1999. Joe invited Helmut and his friends to visit Macari Vineyards, and two years later they offered him the winemaker's position.

"So I started here to make the early wines, first time in 2002, and to make sweet wines, also the ice wine," he explains. "I come back here four times, five times per year, during the harvest, then for stabilization of the wine, before the wine goes to the bottling line, and so on."

The two flying winemakers aren't on the same precise schedule, but their time at Macari overlaps quite a bit. "During harvest we are working together," says Helmut. "She starts one week before, or two weeks before, to get everything ready."

"I stay four months," Paola says, "depending on how it's going."

Paola also works at a winery in Chile. When she returns there, harvest season is about to begin. In spite of the hard work and constant traveling, she loves what she does. "It's very interesting work," Paola explains, "warmer climate and cool climate; there, vinification is different, everything is different. I like it."

Helmut's schedule likewise allows him to be at his vineyard in Austria when needed and in

Mattituck when needed. After the harvest is in and the preliminary winemaking tasks are done at Macari, he says, "I leave, sometimes in the middle of October, and then I come back in the middle of November; then I stay here until a little bit before Christmas; then I go back to Austria again; then come in February and March. Every year we do this. I have two harvest times, different seasons."

He and Paola have been working as a team for five years. "We work on all the white wines and the red wines together," she says. "We decide together." When they're not on the North Fork at the same time, they talk frequently by phone so each knows exactly what the other is doing.

The Wines

Macari Vineyards produces twelve thousand to fourteen thousand cases annually. Whites on the wine list at this writing include Collina 48 Chardonnay, stainless-steel-fermented Chardonnay Estate, Early Wine Chardonnay, Sauvignon Blanc, and oak-aged Chardonnay Reserve.

Reds include Collina 48 Merlot; Merlot Estate; Sette, an equal blend of Merlot and Cabernet Franc; Cabernet Franc; Syrah; Merlot Reserve; and Bergen Road, a Bordeaux blend.

Block E dessert wine was awarded a score of 89 by influential *Wine Spectator* magazine.

Macari Vineyards does not enter many competitions, but when it does, the awards and accolades pour in. Three of its wines won medals in the 2008 National Women's Wine Competition. A gold went to Sauvignon Blanc, silver to the red blend Alexandra, and bronze to Reserve Merlot. No fewer than seven Macari entries won silver medals in the 2007 New York Wine and Food Classic.

Two of Macari's blended red wines have recently

earned superlative reviews: Alexandra and Solo Uno. Solo Uno (Italian for "only one") is the first wine made by Joe Macari Jr.; only 165 cases were produced. According to Alexandra, in a blind tasting against similar wines from California and France, the wine that bears her name came in first.

Macari Vineyards & Winery
150 Bergen Avenue, Mattituck
(631) 298-0100
macari@peconic.net
www.macariwines.com
Open year-round
Owners: The Macari family
Winemakers: Helmut Gangl and Paola Valverde
Founded: 1994
Acres planted: 200
Varieties grown: Chardonnay, Sauvignon Blanc, Viognier, Cabernet Franc, Cabernet Sauvignon, Malbec, Merlot, Petit Verdot, Pinot Noir, Syrah
Long Island Wine Council member
Macari 2: See Cutchogue section

GRILLED THREE-CHEESE SANDWICHES WITH SUNNY SIDE–UP DUCK EGGS

Shinn Estate Farmhouse, Mattituck | *David Page and Barbara Shinn, proprietors*

¼ cup grated cheddar cheese

¼ cup grated Asiago cheese

¼ cup fresh goat cheese curd

3 tablespoons unsalted butter, softened

4 thin slices whole-grain bread

1 medium tomato, thinly sliced

1 tablespoon chopped fresh herbs, plus more for garnish

2 duck eggs

Kosher salt and freshly ground black pepper

1. Combine the cheeses in a small bowl, mixing the grated cheese with the soft goat cheese to form a spread.

2. Lightly butter one side of each slice of bread. Melt 2 teaspoons of the remaining butter in a 10-inch nonstick skillet over medium heat. Place two slices of the bread buttered side down in the skillet; top each slice with the cheese mixture, sliced tomato, and herbs, and place another slice of bread on top, buttered side up. Cook until the sandwiches are golden brown on the bottom, then carefully flip the sandwiches over and brown the other side.

3. While the sandwiches are cooking, preheat oven to 350°F. Place two small, ovenproof skillets over medium heat. When the pans are hot, add 2 teaspoons of butter to each skillet and allow the butter to melt. Crack an egg into each skillet. When the eggs begin to set, transfer the skillets to the hot oven. Allow the eggs to set until the whites are cooked through, about 4 minutes.

4. Place the sandwiches on two warmed plates, top with the eggs, season with salt and pepper, and garnish with herbs.

Serves 2.

LIEB FAMILY CELLARS

LIEB FAMILY CELLARS' TASTING ROOM OCCUPIES A CORNER OF PREMIUM WINE GROUP, THE CUSTOM-CRUSH FACILITY MARK LIEB OWNS with partners Russell Hearn, a winemaker, and Bernard Sussman, Mark's partner in his money-management business.

This is a tasting room with personality. From the green corrugated overhang above the deep red doors in the white-columned entryway to the polished metal tasting tables inside, the look at Lieb Cellars is clean and sleek, with the modern industrial flair of a downtown loft. Exposed air ducts, the same dark red as the doors, and a corrugated silver ceiling continue the theme throughout the room. The effect is completed by a tile floor, a streamlined wall of shelves displaying award-winning wines, and a gleaming, semicircular tasting bar backed by a bank of glass-fronted cubes with interior lighting.

All these shiny surfaces and hard edges might sound uninviting, but the opposite is true. Sunlight filtering through the windows and the soft, golden illumination from the glass-fronted display case behind the bar meld perfectly with the industrial look to lend Lieb Cellars' tasting room a welcoming ambience.

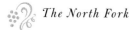

The Owner, Mark Lieb

Mark Lieb owns Lieb Family Cellars with his wife, Kathy. Although he's fully committed to the enterprise, he also runs a money management company called Spectrum Asset Management. So he leaves most of the administration of the wine business to general manager Gary Madden, a Chicago native who arrived on the North Fork by way of California. Gary began by pouring wine in the tasting room, then quickly moved up to management. Kathy used to help out in the business, but now she's involved full-time with the Liebs' two teenage children.

"Gary has really stepped up and taken on a lot of the day-to-day running of the vineyard," Mark tells a visitor to his weekend home beside Lieb Cellars' Cutchogue vineyard. "I'm more on the financial side of it," Mark explains, "but Gary really runs it on a day-to-day basis under my guidance."

When he's asked how he got into the winemaking business, Mark responds, "My father was in the wholesale liquor business when I was growing up in Hartford, Connecticut, in the 1950s and '60s. First it was liquor, and then they started a division selling wine. Every day he'd bring home something different to try. Of course this was in the '50s and '60s—Liebfraumilch and Mateus and all that stuff we grew up with—and I couldn't tell anything about it that was different, but there was always wine on the table.

"So I was exposed to it at a young age," he goes on, "and then, fast-forward, I worked for a company called Drexel Burnham Lambert—Mike Milken, junk bonds, etc.—and spent a fair amount of time in California. I actually lived in California for a while in the 1980s, and I had a very good friend who owned eighty acres in Sonoma that eventually became part of Landmark Vineyards. I spent a lot of time in Sonoma and Napa while I was working at Drexel, and it kind of just gets in your blood and doesn't get out of it."

When Mark left Drexel, he planned to start his money-management firm in St. Helena in Napa Valley, but his future wife balked at moving to earthquake country, so they decided to settle down on the East Coast. With the desire to own a vineyard now firmly entrenched, Mark and Kathy started scouting possible locations.

"We looked in the Hudson Valley and we looked in the Finger Lakes," Mark recounts. "Then I came out here in 1992. The region was having its fits and starts, but I did some homework and saw that there was a lot of good potential."

The Liebs bought twenty acres on Oregon Road in Cutchogue. "Thirteen acres were planted in Pinot Blanc, and then we added more, and added more, and added more," until they had fifty acres of several different varieties. They built a weekend house on the property and sold their grapes to the Lenz Winery and Palmer Vineyards.

"They started winning awards with the grapes," Mark says, "and I thought, 'You know, maybe I should think about this myself,' and I thought about building a small winery. But the economics aren't really there for small wineries. And then Russell Hearn approached me, and that was the birth of Premium Wine Group. So I was able to keep focused on the vineyard and not have to worry about pumps and barrels and tanks and all that stuff, and let Premium do that, which really, I think, makes a lot of sense."

Summing up, Mark says, "So that's kind of where it's grown. Some people here might want to do mass production; some people want to be more specialized. Our venue has always been to sell to the high-end restaurants, which we do, both on the East End and in New York City. We distribute to a couple of different states and we're looking to expand that, but we only make X amount and we want to make it really good." At present "X amount" equals about 7,500 cases; Mark doesn't plan to grow much beyond that.

Mark and Kathy planted their first vines themselves, and Mark is adamant about good vineyard management. "You've got to have really good grapes in the vineyard, because if the grapes are crappy coming out of the vineyard, you're going to have crappy wine. If you try to go cheap in the vineyard, it's going to hurt you.

"And we've all paid our dues, by the way, in learning that process," he says a moment later, referring to his fellow vineyard owners. "This is not like you open up a page of a book and you do this and it's going to come out right. That just doesn't happen."

Warming to the subject of caring for the vines, Mark continues: "There's a lot of things you have to do: Keep them trellised right and pruned right; you've got to spray them right. I mean, you look at a vineyard like this, and I could cut 10 percent in costs right off the top and you wouldn't even see the difference, but it'll start to show up. Not the first year, maybe, but the second year or the third year." Looking out his office window at acres of vines standing stark and bare under a gray April sky, he drives his point home: "There's $10,000 in fertilizer going onto the soil today."

Mark is a big believer in keeping toxic chemicals out of that soil. "We don't use herbicides to control the weeds. I haven't done that in ten years," he says. "All that you see here is in-row tilling, so there's no herbicides on here. People questioned it at the

beginning; we were one of the few. But I noticed— not in one year, but after two, three, four years—that the plants, I felt, were stronger, especially in a couple of weaker spots in the vineyard when I took it over."

As their conversation nears an end, Mark reveals to his guest a surprising fact: He was educated as a meteorologist. "I ended up on Wall Street. That's a long story over many bottles of wine, but I really wanted to work for the National Weather Service," he says.

Next to the huge desk in Mark's home office stands a large, complicated-looking telescope. Now it becomes clear that meteorology is no mere pastime, but a factor in the success of his vineyard.

"It's helped me," Mark says. "I've made some

calls which I think over the years have helped, from picking times to looking at maps and studying what I see. I look at some longer-term maps that I get from the weather service."

Weatherman, finance man, family man, and vineyard owner: Filling all of these roles is a hectic and delicate balancing act, but Mark seems to thrive on it.

The Wines

Lieb Family Cellars' Blanc de Blanc ("white from white"), the sparkling wine made from their Pinot Noir vineyard by Lenz winemaker Eric Fry, has won high acclaim in every vintage. Influential *Wine Spectator* magazine named the 2001 Blanc de Blanc one of the twenty-one Best American Sparkling Wines; the 2002 won double gold and Best in Class at the 2006 L.A. County Fair and International Wine Competition; the 2003 vintage earned a gold medal at the 2007 New York Wine and Food Classic; and the 2004 has already brought home its first medal, a bronze in the 2008 San Francisco Chronicle Wine Competition.

Lieb Cellars' still wines are made at Premium Wine Group under the supervision of Australian winemaker Russell Hearn, who has been making wine on the North Fork for more than twenty years. Mark and Gary work closely with Russell on winemaking decisions.

The current wine list includes many other wines in two basic tiers. All of the reserve wines and nearly all of the second-label wines have won many medals and high praise. The Lieb label appears on its premium line of elegant and complex reserve wines. The Bridge Lane label goes on a line of younger, lighter, "New World–style" wines. Small quantities of rare and specialty wines are also produced.

Whites and rosés on offer as this is written are Bridge Lane Rosé, Bridge Lane White Merlot, Bridge Lane Chardonnay, Reserve Chardonnay, and the company's signature wine, Reserve Pinot Blanc.

In sparkling wines Bridge Lane Bubbly and Blanc de Blanc are on the current wine list.

Reds include Bridge Lane Cabernet Franc, Bridge Lane Merlot, Reserve Cabernet Franc, Reserve Merlot, and a Meritage Bordeaux blend.

Two specialty wines are currently produced. September's Mission Merlot is priced at $9.11; 10 percent of the retail price goes to the September's Mission Foundation, which funds projects honoring the victims of the 2001 terrorist attacks. Syrah, a new release in May 2008, is named for Lieb Cellars' cherished canine mascot, who died in 2007. For every bottle of Syrah purchased, 20 percent of the retail price is donated to the nonprofit Animal Medical Center in New York City for research and treatment of kidney disease in animals.

Lieb Family Cellars
35 Cox Neck Road, Mattituck
(631) 298-1942
info@liebcellars.com
www.liebcellars.com
Open year-round
Owners: Mark and Kathy Lieb
Winemaker: Premium Wine Group
Founded: 1992
Acres planted: 50
Varieties grown: Chardonnay, Pinot Blanc, Cabernet Franc, Cabernet Sauvignon, Malbec, Merlot, Petit Verdot
Long Island Wine Council member

SHINN ESTATE VINEYARDS

A VISIT TO SHINN ESTATE VINEYARDS IS A TRIP BACK IN TIME, TO AN ERA BEFORE THE NORTH FORK BECAME THE POPULAR TOURIST destination it is today. Oregon Road, which briefly parallels the two main east-west routes, offers a precious glimpse into the living agricultural heritage of Long Island. No store, no gas station, no housing development mars its green and peaceful beauty. David Page and Barbara Shinn, the husband-and-wife owners of Shinn Estate, are doing all they can to keep it that way.

A lovingly and elegantly restored historic farmhouse is the first thing you see as you approach the vineyard. This is Shinn Estate Farmhouse, a four-bedroom bed-and-breakfast where all the meals are prepared with local ingredients by David, an accomplished chef. Willing guests are put to work in the vineyard during Wine Asylum Weekends.

Around back, a stone's throw from the fifteen-acre vineyard, is a small tasting room with glass-topped wrought-iron tables and woven-mat chairs that somehow manages to seem rustic and upscale at the same time. In the summer a bench just outside the door holds a selection of broad-brimmed straw hats for vineyard walks. Monarchs and tiger swallowtails flutter around the many butterfly bushes, and a lush trumpet vine drapes its fiery blossoms across the roof beams of an inviting patio.

Contiguous with the tasting room is a soaring restored barn that houses the gleaming stainless-steel tanks of the estate's winery. Another barn across the way has been converted to house French oak barrels and a private tasting room.

The Owners, Barbara Shinn and David Page

In 1994, standing in the basement wine cellar of one of the Manhattan restaurants he ran with Barbara Shinn, David Page said to himself, "Wouldn't it be great to have a bottle of wine with our own name on it to serve in the restaurant?" They had always promoted Long Island wines, so it wasn't a big jump from that thought to working with East End growers to make their own wine.

Four years later, Barbara and David were managing four businesses and thinking of starting a fifth when they pulled up short and took a long, hard look at what they were doing. Their soul-searching led them to choose a different kind of life, one connected to the land. Keeping the original Greenwich Village restaurant, Home, they divested themselves of the rest and began looking for land on the North Fork. They have since sold that restaurant, too, fully committing themselves to their new way of life.

"In the city we were pale-skinned, staying up late," David recalls, "but here we see the sunrise and sunset every day. It's a smarter way to live one's life. You go to bed early and turn off the lights. It saves energy."

Saving energy—indeed, everything green—is vitally important to the couple. Sustainable vineyard practices are the norm at Shinn Estate; they use only organic nutrients and fertilizers. No herbicides are allowed, and they never cultivate the soil between the rows. The daisies that grow there go into liquid compost that is run through the drip irrigation system to return natural nutrients to the soil.

"Soil is an incubator," says David. "Compost encourages all the bacteria and fungi that keep soil healthy throughout the life cycle. It creates all the nutrients plants need. You don't need a fifty-pound bag of fertilizer. We started the soil work in 1998, and we're now starting to see dramatic results."

Barbara Shinn

To Barbara and David, grape farming is about patience, meticulous care, and creative problem solving. "The joy and happiness come from problem solving," David comments. "It's trying to get clear with the vineyard so you don't destroy habitat."

"You have to look at a farm as a place of peacefulness," adds Barbara. "Enter that frame of thought, and inevitably your touch will be gentle. That's where good farming practices start. It's not about being at war with insects and weather. You still make the same decisions as others, but you take a different approach and come up with different solutions."

"Barbara comes from an art background," David notes. "She's very creative. Something is lost when it's being done more by recipe than by that kind of instinct. Great things come out of creative endeavor. That's a big part of what we do here, at great risk. You have to be creative, think outside the box, and it doesn't always work. That can be very depressing. It's blood, sweat, and tears: Farming equals all of that."

Barbara, an Ohio native who holds a master's degree in fine art, laughs as she adds, "I'm pretty good at creative problem solving—and creative problem making! David will tell you that."

David grew up in Wisconsin, where there's still a great deal of land in farming and every youth spends time on a farm. "It was just what you did. You planted a garden, even in town. Everyone worked on farms. Did you know the school year was established so children could spend time on the farm?"

He's adamant about teaching people the origins of the food they eat. "Americans have lost the ability to comprehend what farming is," he says. "Less than 2 percent of Americans now farm. We need to get our youth back onto farms, get them thinking about what we eat. They don't know where their food comes from."

Barbara and David know where their food comes from, and their wine. "Wine is such an important thing—drinking it, enjoying it," Barbara says. But it's also about caring for our baby vines, being stewards of the land, leaving it in better shape than when we found it."

The Wines

Shinn Estate's wines have won wide acclaim since their first vintage, a result the owners attribute to their careful attention to every detail. "Barbara and I are some of the most meticulous growers on Long Island," David notes. "We're really careful about not having debris during fermentation, like leaves, or over- or underripe berries. We remove debris in the vineyard."

David, who's been a professional chef for more than thirty years, thinks winemakers, like chefs, get too much credit for the finished product. "The chef's job is not to mess it up, not to add one too many things. Ingredients need to be handled carefully. It's the same way in the winery. Tech people don't make wine; it's grown, not made."

He and Barbara give their winemaker, Anthony Nappa, the right ingredients; then they participate fully in determining each wine's style and deciding on the final blend.

Shinn Estate produces six thousand cases a year, generally in small lots that sell out quickly. Currently these include a table wine called Red; Nine Barrel Reserve Merlot, the estate's signature red; Estate Merlot; Cabernet Franc; a red blend playfully named Wild Boar Doe; Coalescence, a white blend; "first-fruit" Sauvignon Blanc Semillon; "bone dry" Rosé; steel-fermented Chardonnay; and Shinn Estate Vineyards Brut, a Champagne-style sparkler made by Gilles Martin. A new release is a sparkling wine made entirely from Chardonnay.

Shinn Estate Vineyards
2000 Oregon Road, Mattituck
(631) 804-0367
shinnvin@optonline.net
www.shinnestatevineyards.com
www.shinnfarmhouse.com
Open year-round
Owners: Barbara Shinn and David Page
Winemaker: Anthony Nappa
Founded: 1998
Acres planted: 22
Varieties grown: Pinot Blanc, Sauvignon Blanc, Cabernet Franc, Cabernet Sauvignon, Malbec, Merlot, Petit Verdot
Long Island Wine Council member

SHERWOOD HOUSE VINEYARDS

ORTH OF ROUTE 48 IN MATTITUCK, ELIJAH'S LANE CUTS THROUGH ACRES OF FARMLAND ON ITS WAY TO OREGON ROAD. Soon you'll see a vineyard on your left. Drive slowly, or you might miss the entrance to Sherwood House Vineyards. Turning in, you'll find you're in an avenue of vines leading arrow-straight to the tiniest tasting room you're ever likely to see.

What started out as a storage shed designed to look like a miniature barn has been transformed with taste and ingenuity into a cottage straight out of a fairy tale. You can almost imagine coming upon it in the woods and trying to guess what delightful, diminutive soul lives there from the straw hats hanging on the door, the bright red blankets draped over woven picnic baskets, and the artfully arranged pots of colorful flowers.

And as if the cottage itself weren't inviting enough, picnic tables shaded by green umbrellas beckon visitors to linger a while, sipping wine, chatting with the pourer—who just might be one of the owners—and enjoying the company of their dogs: miniature poodle Rufus, toy poodle Raven, shitzupoo Roger, and bichon frise Radish.

The Owners, Dr. Charles and Barbara Smithen
Charles and Barbara Smithen had owned a house on Long Island Sound in Peconic for twenty years before they decided to buy land and plant a vineyard. Each had a successful career in New York City.

Charles, tall, trim, and white-haired, is a world-renowned cardiologist and cardiac surgeon who says he's "semiretired—I think!" A native of Canada, he was on the staff of New York Presbyterian Hospital and an assistant professor at Cornell Medical School.

Barbara, a still-beautiful former Manhattan Debutante of the Year who once graced the cover of *Town & Country* magazine, worked in financial public relations. While she was growing up, her parents had a house in the Hamptons. "Very posh,"

she says, "ball gowns and everything." Always the adventurous type, in her youth Barbara raced big sailboats out of Manhattan.

Her father, Hugh Owen, was vice president of Paramount Pictures in the late 1950s and early 1960s. "He made Elvis movies, *Ben Hur*, Doris Day movies, *Breakfast at Tiffany's*," she recalls. "I got to meet Elvis, and I cut the cake at the premiere of *A Hard Day's Night*. I didn't want to go to the Beatles concert, but Dad insisted, and I screamed the loudest!"

Reflecting on the distance between the debutante balls of her youth and her present life on the North Fork, Barbara says, "Now I'm a farm girl. My sister has a horse farm, and my mother asks how she ended up with two farm girls."

Charles's appreciation for wine goes way back, but the real love affair began while he was in London doing medical research in the late 1960s. Whenever he got the chance, he crossed the Channel to France to visit the different wine regions, tasting, observing, and learning. He became a passionate collector of fine wines and now has a collection of Armagnac going back to 1907, along with what he calls "my own stash" of wines from 1942, the year of his birth.

He also has a collection of antique corkscrews, one as old as 1690. The corkscrew depicted on the vineyard's classically French-style wine label is one of only three like it in the world.

Three decades after Charles's youthful sojourn in London, the Smithens sold some property in New York City and asked themselves what they wanted to do with the proceeds. "I said, 'No more cement!'" Barbara declares.

Her fervent desire to leave the city behind and their shared passion for the vineyards and wines of France led Charles into a rather extravagant impulse

purchase one day in 1996. He called Barbara in the city and told her to come to the North Fork because he was going to look at some land. Barbara smiles with a kind of wide-eyed, nostalgic astonishment as she remembers the moment. "I got off the bus, and Charles told me, 'We bought a farm!' "

Recovering from her initial shock as she marveled at a rose garden with blooms "the size of dinner plates," and realizing the potential in the classic 1860 farmhouse, Barbara fell in love with the farm that was to become Sherwood House Vineyards.

The Smithens hired local expert Steve Mudd to plant their vineyard with clones of the highest quality French vines.

Both Charles and Barbara say a big part of their reason for starting Sherwood House was that it was something they could do as a couple. "We're passionate about everything we do," Charles says,

"and we wanted to do something together. This is a beautiful second career, different from what we both did. The North Fork was the perfect setting to start our vineyard; it's so rewarding, drinking our wine."

"We were so excited about our first vines," Barbara recalls. "We're having so much fun." They love taking their dogs for sunset rides in the vineyard on their golf cart. "They won't let us go without them," Barbara says.

When a guest asks what they do on their annual visits to France, Charles laughs with delight as he details their simple itinerary: "We eat, we drink wine, and we visit vineyards! We've visited Burgundy, southern Provence, Côtes du Rhone . . ." It's clear he could go on and on.

Since they spend so much time in the south of France, they decided to get their own place there. "We've bought a little house in Antibes," Barbara says, "a fisherman's house on ramparts. It's on the street where Napoleon's sister lived, and it still has Roman baths. The owners used to sell anchovies and olive oil," she relates, obviously enchanted with her new home away from home.

The Winemaker, Gilles Martin, and the Wines

For the first three years after their vines began producing fruit, the Smithens sold their grapes to local wineries. When they were ready to launch their own label, they hired a highly experienced and respected French winemaker, Gilles Martin. Charles wanted to make fine white wines in the style of the Burgundy region, wines like the famous Puligny-Montrachet, made from the Chardonnay grape.

Gilles fit in perfectly with their plans; he was educated at Montpellier, the famous viticultural school in the south of France, and has made some of the best-known white Burgundies in the world, including Châteauneuf du Pape. He has worked at highly respected wineries around the world, in Germany, Australia, and Roederer Estate in California, famed for its sparkling wines. No stranger to the Long Island wine region, Gilles made wine for Macari and Martha Clara vineyards, then spent some time at a winery in Virginia before returning to Long Island.

The first release from Sherwood House, the 1999 Chardonnay, won a bronze medal at one of the most prestigious contests in the world, the International Wine Challenge in London. Sherwood House wines continue to reap gold, silver, and bronze medals in a wide array of competitions. In a Miami competition Sherwood House entries won in nine out of twelve categories. The 2001 Chardonnay took a gold in the New York Wine and Food Classic, and the 2001 Merlot also earned a gold in the L.A. County Fair Wines of the World competition.

Sherwood House Vineyards makes only a few wines, usually offering them in several vintages. Chardonnay, Oregon Road Merlot, and the premium Sherwood House Merlot are currently on the wine list, along with a third Merlot called Merliance. Merliance is a collaboration among the five members of the Long Island Merlot Alliance. Formed to promote Merlot as the region's signature grape, LIMA sponsors research, development, and education aimed at maintaining and improving the quality of the region's Merlot. LIMA members—Sherwood House, Shinn Estate, Raphael, Pellegrini, and Wölffer Estate—each contribute two barrels to the blend of 100 percent Merlot.

Sherwood House Vineyards
2600 Oregon Road, Mattituck
(631) 298-1396
info@sherwoodhousevineyards.com
www.sherwoodhousevineyards.com
Tasting house: Elijah's Lane
Open May through November
Sherwood House wines are also sold at the Tasting Room (see Peconic section). A second tasting room may be open by the time of publication; call or check the Web site for details.
Owners: Charles and Barbara Smithen
Winemaker: Gilles Martin
Founded: 1996
Acres planted: 38
Varieties grown: Chardonnay, Cabernet Franc, Cabernet Sauvignon, Merlot, Petit Verdot
Long Island Wine Council member

PELLEGRINI VINEYARDS

PELLEGRINI VINEYARDS SITS ON A KNOLL, LOOKING OUT OVER A GREEN SLOPE OF LAWN AND ROW UPON ROW OF GRAPEVINES ACROSS THE MAIN ROAD. ON one side of its white-columned courtyard stands a tall, windowed tower, on the other, a two-story structure with a wide-peaked roof. Add cedar shingles, white trim, and a dark green roof, and the overall effect is one of clean-lined, modern elegance informed by a deep respect for traditional North Fork architecture.

Inside the tasting room, with its open beams and dark tile floor, a vaulted ceiling rises to the full height of the tower, and stairs lead to a mezzanine offering a view of the vineyard across the road and the tasting room below. On clear, warm days the large courtyard is a popular place to sit and sip your wine.

Just beyond the courtyard is the entrance to the winery wing, where large glass windows allow a view into the winery below. A covered walkway leads from the courtyard to an open deck with a close-up view of the vineyard. From there you might glimpse a white gazebo on a stretch of grass between the vines.

The Owners, Bob and Joyce Pellegrini

Bob Pellegrini owns a successful graphic design business in New York City; his wife, Joyce, is a retired schoolteacher. On a blustery day in March,

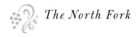

they sit with a guest in an upstairs room overlooking the vineyard to talk about their adventures in the wine trade.

"We've done an unbelievable job here," Bob begins, referring to the whole Long Island wine industry. "I first came out here in the early 1980s, and never, ever did I think that this industry would grow the way it has. It started out more as a dream—well, it still is—and a hope, and something serious to do that I loved, yet I never thought that it would turn into what it is."

Bob didn't set out to own a vineyard and winery. His journey began with a general interest in wine, then expanded to joining wine clubs, collecting fine wine, and installing a wine cellar to hold his collection. In truth, his love affair with wine started long before

that, while he was growing up in the Bronx with parents who were first-generation Americans.

"My father was born here, but his family moved back to Italy when he was three," Bob says. "Then the family came back here when he was in his twenties. My mother was born here. My grandparents were all born in Italy."

"And didn't speak English," Joyce comments.

"I was raised in an Italian family where family was everything," Bob resumes, "and food was important, and the gathering of family and friends around food and wine was part of the culture. That's the way I was brought up, having a glass in front of me—not every day, of course, but on special occasions. They poured a little wine and water, and then, as I got older, there was more wine and less water."

Many years later, like a number of others who eventually staked a claim in the region, he became intrigued by reports of the vineyards on the North Fork.

"Joyce and I came out here at the beginning of all this and said, 'Gee, it would be a really nice thing to do,'" Bob recounts. "Again, I never thought it would be at this scale. We were looking for a ten- to fifteen-acre farm, a place to go on weekends—sort of a dream, without any real concept of . . ."

"It was like a grownup retirement thing to do," Joyce interjects.

"Or eventual retirement," Bob responds. "Retirement's a long word; I never use that word. Anyway, whether it was going to be commercial or not, whether it was going to be an economic success or not, was not really the initial impetus. But when we looked into it and realized it had to be a certain size and a certain volume to even be able to buy a tractor or pay for a vineyard manager and so forth, then it became a reality.

"That's how it started," he continues, "and then one thing led to another, and fortunately my New York business did very well and I was able to afford what I have."

Then, with perfect comedic timing, Bob adds with a laugh, "I still have my New York business to be able to afford what I have."

The first vines were planted on the property in 1982, about ten years before the Pellegrinis bought it. "When we first came out here," Bob explains, "this front block was already planted. Now we own not just this vineyard; we own three other properties down the road. We own another forty acres in Peconic and another sixteen acres in Southold. We now have ninety acres in total, and I think about seventy are actually planted and in production at this point."

In the early days Joyce and Bob worked in the vineyards themselves. Joyce taught in elementary schools in Harlem and the South Bronx for twenty years. By the time she retired in 1991, she was a reading specialist. When her guest remarks how tough her job must have been, Joyce responds, "There's not a lot of help around for you at all. All I know is, when I retired and came out here and tied vines, I thought, 'They're quiet! I hear birds singing!' It was wonderful."

"It was a very romantic and satisfying experience, it really was," adds Bob.

"We tied, Bob plowed, Bob sprayed—we were really active in the vineyard," Joyce says, then adds in a playfully wistful tone, "That's when we were younger."

A moment later, describing what it was like to work in the vineyard, Joyce says, "It gets almost meditative, because you do the same thing, and after a while your mind just stops and you just do it. . . ."

"In general," Bob says, "the wine business has all those things we just talked about, all the romantic aspects of it, the pleasurable part. But it's also a business, and the alcohol business, at least in this part of the country, I guess, is a very difficult thing."

Deeper into the conversation, Bob returns to one of the chief challenges of the wine business: keeping up with the voluminous tangle of regulations. "I would say that we have a full-time person—it's split up between a couple of different people—that does nothing but the paperwork," he declares. "Just the compliance with the New York State Liquor Authority, the compliance with the BATF [Bureau of Alcohol, Tobacco, and Firearms], just to keep all the records that they require.

"You do this for the love of it," he adds. "Fortunately, we've been involved with Russell Hearn—to me the best winemaker out here—who started with us and still is involved on a very, very intimate level. We hired him before we actually built the winery, in the planning process. And then of course when it was built we did our first vintage here, which was 1992."

Asked to talk about that first vintage, Bob replies with enthusiasm. "We were absolutely thrilled and excited, and again there was the expectation that we were going to make one of the best wines out here, and we feel we still do—to me we're in the top rank. In the beginning it was a rush, it really was. It was a very exciting time."

He says he knew virtually nothing about making wine, except what he'd read in books, when he started Pellegrini Vineyards. Instead of trying to learn the ropes by himself, he applied the business philosophy he says has served him well over the years: When you want to do something right and you don't have the knowledge and skills it takes, hire a professional. He repeats this mantra with a hearty laugh.

"One of the reasons why I chose Russell," he goes on, "is we got along real well and we had a similar kind of palate. Right away, from day one—and this was in the days when California Chardonnays were nothing but oak—right off the bat we both said, 'Now, wait a minute!' Because he showed me his favorite Chardonnay, and I pulled out my favorite Chardonnay, and they were similar. They were fruit-driven, not overly oaked or not that big, buttery

kind of showy wine. So we started off real well that way. We both had the same idea of what a real wine should be."

"Bob and Russell meet every Monday," Joyce says. "They do blendings; they test wines—Russell keeps Bob very much up to date on what's going on and what to taste and what to do."

The Winemaker, Russell Hearn

Russell Hearn is from Australia, but he's been on the North Fork since 1990.

"It's been quite a while," he says in his distinctive accent. "I started in the wine industry there. I worked for a winery called Horton in western Australia; they were owned by the Hardys group. After about five years I did an exchange to the States, to work briefly at a winery out west, and then came to visit a girl on the East Coast for what was supposed to be six weeks."

Twenty-three years later, Russell and the girl he came to see—and later married—are still here. "She's from Massachusetts," Russell recounts, "so we looked on the East Coast to see what we thought was the best area for personal reasons as well as professional reasons, and Long Island definitely is that."

He's as enthusiastic as are Bob and Joyce about his involvement with Pellegrini Vineyards. "I got involved with Pellegrini right at the beginning," he says. "Before there was a winery, I was lucky enough to be involved in the design and construction phase, so I guess you could say I was employee number one. I came in before the bricks and mortar.

"I was there full-time from 1992, with their first vintage, through 2000," Russell continues. "And in 2000 I evolved to being a very actively involved consulting winemaker, and my other role is now at

Premium Wine Group," he says, referring to the custom-crush winemaking facility in Mattituck, which he owns in partnership with Lieb Family Cellars owner Mark Lieb and Mark's partner in his financial management business, Bernard Sussman.

"But I'm still very much the winemaker at Pellegrini Vineyards," Russell says. "The Pellegrinis and I want our arrangement to continue a long, long time, so I plan on being the winemaker there ten years from now, fifteen years from now."

The Wines
Russell and Bob agree that they want to make wines with true varietal characteristics. "We want to make sure our Merlot tastes like Merlot and our Cabernet Franc tastes like Cabernet Franc," says Bob. "That's the main thing we look for; that and the flavor and the taste of the wine, really, is what we go for, and to make sure that it's not too acidic, it's well rounded and so forth."

Consistency between vintages is also an important goal at Pellegrini Vineyards. They often accomplish this, like most other wineries, by blending in small amounts of other varietals, being careful not to exceed the limit imposed by New York State law, which mandates that at least 85 percent of varietal-labeled wines must be that varietal.

But Pellegrini Vineyards also ventures beyond varietals to make a premium red blend called Encore. "We both believe that sometimes the best wines we do are blends that don't particularly meet a varietal rule," Bob says.

"Our main goal is to keep the consistency, to make sure that our customers are happy," he adds a little later. "That's kind of the motivation, and we do the best we can each year. That's really it. We don't make a mystery out of it, you know. Wine is to be enjoyed. We don't want to hype our wines, that's the main thing. We want to be as honest and straightforward as possible. There's so much about the snob appeal, and I don't buy it at all."

Pellegrini Vineyards' wines are divided into three tiers: The East End Select label goes on fresh, crisp, light- to medium-bodied table wines; the Pellegrini Vineyards label appears on medium- to full-bodied oak-aged wines; and the Vintner's Pride label denotes full-bodied, premium wines made from the finest estate-grown fruit.

The East End Select label currently offers Chardonnay, Rosé of Cabernet Sauvignon, and Merlot. Wines with the Pellegrini Vineyards imprint include Chardonnay, Cabernet Franc, Cabernet Sauvignon, and Merlot. Vintner's Pride Merlot and Vintner's Pride Finale Bin 1333, a dessert wine, appear on the tasting list as of this writing.

Special limited-production wines are sometimes available to wine club members.

Pellegrini Vineyards
23005 Main Road, Cutchogue
(631) 734-4111
wine@pellegrinivineyards.com
www.pellegrinivineyards.com
Open year-round
Owners: Bob and Joyce Pellegrini
Winemaker: Russell Hearn
Founded: 1991
Acres planted: 70
Varieties grown: Chardonnay, Sauvignon Blanc, Gewürztraminer, Cabernet Franc, Cabernet Sauvignon, Merlot, Petit Verdot
Long Island Wine Council member

MACARI 2

TWO STATELY STONE PILLARS MARK THE ENTRANCE TO MACARI 2, THE SECOND TASTING ROOM OF MACARI VINEYARDS & WINERY in Mattituck. At the end of the long driveway, at the top of a hill, stands a structure that looks like a country manor. The double doors, wide veranda, and brick chimney all add to the feeling that you're about to enter someone's gracious home.

The ambience continues inside the large, airy tasting room, where wines made at the Mattituck facility are available for tasting and purchase.

For more information about Macari Vineyards & Winery, see the Mattituck section. For more information about Macari 2, call or visit the Web site.

Macari 2
Main Road, Cutchogue
(631) 298-0100
macari@peconic.net
www.macariwines.com
Open year-round
Long Island Wine Council member

CASTELLO DI BORGHESE VINEYARD & WINERY

AN ANCIENT FARM TRUCK SITS ON THE LAWN IN FRONT OF CASTELLO DI BORGHESE, ITS FLATBED STACKED WITH OLD WINE BARRELS. Large white letters on the ends of the barrels spell out messages to passersby on Route 48, known to locals as the North Road. As this is written, the message is PINOT NOIR.

The Castello di Borghese tasting room, by outward appearances a simple, low-slung, unassuming building, offers surprises beyond the door. On your left as you pass beyond the heavy wooden door is the tasting room and gift shop, a dark-paneled, elegant space graced by French doors overlooking the vineyard.

But the real surprise lies beyond the spacious terra-cotta-tiled entry hall: A cavernous converted barn, a barrel storage room before the reign of its current owners, Marco and Ann Marie Borghese, has been turned into a gallery and performance space where art adorns the walls and music often fills the air.

This landmark vineyard holds the oldest vines on eastern Long Island. They were planted by

Long Island's wine country pioneers, Louisa and Alex Hargrave, in 1973. The original seventeen acres of Cabernet Sauvignon have expanded to eighty-five acres planted in Pinot Noir, Cabernet Franc, Cabernet Sauvignon, Merlot, Chardonnay, Sauvignon Blanc, and Riesling.

The Owners, Marco and Ann Marie Borghese

Marco Borghese is tall man whose ruggedly handsome, patrician face and distinctive accent are telling: He's an Italian prince whose royal lineage can be traced to the ninth century. Until you get to know him, Marco can seem quiet, even shy, but then his genuine smile, easy laugh, and self-deprecating sense of humor reveal his true personality. Ann Marie, with her petite stature, fair coloring, and outgoing demeanor, makes for a sharp contrast to

her husband. The story of how these two seeming opposites came together shares a lot in common with the classic children's tale "Country Mouse and City Mouse."

Marco grew up on a farm his grandmother managed in the "absolute country" outside Florence. When his grandmother died the family moved to Rome, where they were originally from. After Marco graduated from the University of Rome, his father sent him to the United States so he could attend MIT. "He was a frustrated engineer," jokes Marco. "After six months I went back to Italy knowing English, more or less." But he had fallen in love with New York City, so when the opportunity arose, he returned and stayed.

His father sent some of the things Marco had left behind by way of a friend in Philadelphia; eventually that friend became Marco's partner in opening China to trade with the United States. "We were kind of pioneers in that business," Marco says. "I was one of the first to go to China."

Ann Marie was a city girl from Wilmington, Delaware, who, she declares, "had never spent a night in the country in my life" before moving to the North Fork. Fulfilling a childhood dream likely inspired by her love of British rock bands, she toured Europe on her own at age sixteen. After high school she lived in Paris on and off for a few years, also spending a lot of time in Rome. "After that I went to college at the University of Delaware," Ann Marie says, "and then I moved to Philadelphia and met Marco."

Ann Marie Borghese prepares dessert for a wine dinner at home.

It wasn't a chance meeting. Having experienced Europe, Ann Marie thought she might like to live and work in Asia, so a mutual friend introduced her to Marco. But by that time, the "big boys" had taken over the business, Marco says. "China became too big for our britches," he says with a laugh.

On a rainy Thanksgiving weekend in 1998, the Borgheses were staying with friends in the Hamptons when someone suggested they all go to the North Fork to taste wine.

"I didn't know the North Fork was making wine," Marco admits, "but we visited a few wineries, and this was one of the ones we visited."

He was impressed by the quality of the wine and the beauty of the North Fork, so when he heard that Hargrave Vineyard was up for sale, being between business opportunities, Marco was intrigued. One thing led to another and, as Ann Marie likes to tell it, "He said he'd bought it. I thought he meant the bottle; he meant the vineyard!"

Marco laughs when his wife offers her

abbreviated version. "Believe it or not," he asserts, "I did discuss it with my darling wife!"

A year later he was on-site, but it took Ann Marie six more months to get used to the idea of living in the country. "The transition was much more complex and complicated for me than it was for Marco and the two children," she said. "There was no connection to my previous life."

When she finally arrived, she set about re-creating part of that previous life by making Castello di Borghese a "cultural destination," complete with art shows, live music, opera, and other events.

Like many new vineyard owners, the Borgheses had a romantic notion of the lifestyle. "It seemed like a good way to spend some of my days," Marco says. Instead, he found he had suddenly become a farmer, with all the hard work, crucial decision-making, and weather worries farming entails.

"Marco thought he was going to be a gentleman farmer," adds Ann Marie. "Instead he became a gentleman farming."

Marco Borghese enjoys cooking for guests.

Ann Marie leads frequent walks through the vineyard, explaining to visitors the business of making wine. "When they see how much work it actually takes to get wine into the bottle, people are astounded," she says. She also takes pleasure in teaching people how to pair wine with food and has written a cookbook on the subject, with the proceeds benefiting the Association for the Help of Retarded Children.

In spite of all the hard work and uncertainty, the Borgheses find great satisfaction in what they're doing. They enjoy the artful science of winemaking and the excitement and challenge of coaxing each vintage into the best wine it can be.

"I do happen to like it," Marco says. "Growing grapes is like growing babies: It's very rewarding when you achieve results."

The Wines

The Borgheses serve as their own winemakers, working with consultants for the different varietals. "It's been a great joy to have time in the cellar," says Ann Marie, "working with different people, knowing what we want and seeing it come to fruition."

Their shared goal is to craft elegant, well-balanced, French-style wines that reflect their *terroir* and the best characteristics of each varietal, and that age with grace.

Castello di Borghese's wines have won high praise from wine critics and numerous awards in international competitions. The 2004 Pinot Noir, the winery's signature red varietal, won silver medals in the 2008 Finger Lakes International Wine Competition and the 2007 Great New York State Fair, where the 2001 Reserve Merlot also earned a silver medal. A bronze medal went to the 2004 Cabernet Franc at the State Fair, and the 2006 Sauvignon Blanc won bronze medals in both the Finger Lakes and State Fair competitions.

The winery also currently produces Meritage and Private Reserve blends, Riesling, and a dessert wine made from Chardonnay.

Castello di Borghese Vineyard & Winery
17150 Route 48, Cutchogue
(631) 734-5111
info@castellodiborghese.com
www.borghesevineyard.com
Open year-round
Owners/winemakers: Marco and Ann Marie Borghese
Founded: 1973 (as Hargrave Vineyard)
Acres planted: 85
Varieties grown: Chardonnay, Cabernet Franc, Riesling, Merlot, Sauvignon Blanc, Pinot Noir
Long Island Wine Council member

VINEYARD 48

VINEYARD 48'S TWO-STORY, FOUR-SQUARE TASTING ROOM IS LIKE NONE OTHER ON THE EAST END. BUILT BY ITS ORIGINAL OWNERS in the early 1980s, it was bought along with the vineyard by a group of relatives in the spring of 2004: the Bortone, Lamanna, Metz, and Pipia families.

Visitors are greeted by a striking, diamond-shaped sign on Route 48, which, of course, gives the winery its unusual and catchy name. Inside, a high ceiling and wraparound windows fill the large, airy space with light. The tasting bar, with its almost art deco style, and an exposed silver-colored air duct running around the room and through the corner columns complete the ultramodern look. The floor is tiled in warm shades of terra-cotta and gold, and work by local artists adorns the walls; small tables and chairs offer tasters a place to relax.

Outside, a brick patio and picnic area that occupies the space between the tasting room and the winery invites guests to linger over their wine at one of Vineyard 48's many special events.

Co-owner Rose Pipia
Although several related families own Vineyard 48 together, the dream at its heart belonged to Rose Pipia. Born into a winemaking family in a small

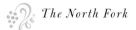

village in the Agrigento province of Sicily, Rose came by her love of the vineyard life naturally.

"All my life, my family was in the wine business," she tells a visitor to Vineyard 48's tasting room. "The winemaking system was completely different there," she adds. "It was all was done by hand, in small containers. Now, here, we have the machines, French oak and everything."

From their four-hundred-acre vineyard, Rose's family produced white wines from grapes in the Riesling family and full-bodied, "robusto" red table wines.

In 1961, when she was nineteen and newly married, Rose immigrated with her husband to New York City, where the young couple settled in Queens. Both of them obtained skilled work in New York City's Garment District. While Rose cut patterns

and stitched glamorous evening attire for wealthy women, her husband was hired by the top designers of the time.

Through all the years in New York City, as her own family grew, Rose never forgot her love for life on the family vineyard back in Sicily. After her husband's passing in 1991 and her own retirement a number of years later, Rose's dream became stronger and stronger.

Finally, in 2003, with her sons, she began to look in eastern Long Island's wine region for a place to make her dream come true. As it happened, Bidwell Vineyards was on the market at the time. After they saw the property on Route 48 in Cutchogue and fell in love with it, Rose and her sons decided the time had come to reclaim their winemaking heritage.

With initial help from her son Joseph, Rose

hired two experts: vineyard manager Steve Mudd, of Mudd Vineyards, to advise them about the existing vineyard and planting new vines, and master winemaker Roman Roth, of Wölffer Estate Vineyard and his own label, The Grapes of Roth, to consult on making the wine. They helped decide what to do with the wine that was still in tanks and barrels and how best to rejuvenate parts of the vineyard.

New barrels and winemaking equipment were purchased, and eventually the Pipias appointed experienced North Fork winemaker Matthew Berenz, who had previously worked at Pindar Vineyards, as Vineyard 48's full-time winemaker.

The new owners have planted several more acres in Riesling, Sauvignon Blanc, Chardonnay, Cabernet Sauvignon, Merlot, and Cabernet Franc.

There's something at Vineyard 48 that visitors won't find anywhere else in the Long Island wine region: a cigar factory. Right next to the tasting room is a small stucco building called the Little Cigar Factory, where handcrafted and custom cigars are available.

Reserve, Cabernet Sauvignon Reserve, Cabernet Franc, and the company's premier red blend, Vignetta ("Little Vineyard") Meritage.

Peach and pumpkin wines are currently produced under the NoFo label.

The Wines

With some of the older vines on the North Fork, planted in 1982, Vineyard 48 has an apt motto: "New wines from old vines." Working with fruit from these mature vines and younger ones planted by the Pipias, winemaker Matthew Berenz produces wines that have won consistent praise for their high quality and Italian-style food-friendliness since the first releases in 2005. The winery makes about six thousand cases of wine a year.

In whites Vineyard 48 currently produces Chardonnay, Chardonnay Reserve, Sauvignon Blanc, Riesling, and White Table Wine.

Reds include Red Table Wine, Merlot, Merlot

Vineyard 48
18910 Route 48, Cutchogue
(631) 734-5200
info@vineyard48winery.com
www.vineyard48winery.com
Open year-round
Owners: The Bortone, Lamanna, Metz, and Pipia families
Winemaker: Matthew Berenz
Founded: 1982 (as Bidwell Vineyards)
Acres planted: 28
Varieties grown: Chardonnay, Riesling, Sauvignon Blanc, Cabernet Franc, Cabernet Sauvignon, Merlot
Long Island Wine Council member

SEARED DUCK BREAST WITH CITRUS GLAZE

Jedediah Hawkins Inn, Jamesport | *Michael Ross and Tom Schaudel, chefs*

4 duck breasts*
2 tablespoons chopped thyme
2 tablespoons marjoram
1 tablespoon olive oil
2 oranges, sectioned
1 grapefruit, sectioned
½ cup sugar
2 tablespoons water
1 teaspoon light corn syrup
¼ cup Champagne vinegar
1 quart tangerine juice
Arrowroot to thicken

*Chefs Ross and Schaudel
recommend duck from Jurgielewicz
Farms in Moriches.

1. Combine duck breasts, chopped thyme and marjoram, and olive oil in a nonreactive bowl and toss to coat duck. Marinate in the refrigerator for 2–3 hours.
2. Preheat oven to 350°F . In a nonstick pan sear duck breasts, skin side down, over medium heat for 6–8 minutes, until the skin is crisp and golden brown in color. Turn the breasts over and place in the oven for an additional 5 minutes. Remove the breasts from the pan and let them rest at room temperature for 5 minutes before slicing.
3. Combine orange and grapefruit sections, sugar, water, and corn syrup in a saucepot. Cook over low heat, stirring until sugar is dissolved. Then cook until golden brown without stirring.
4. Remove sauce from the heat; add Champagne vinegar and 3 cups tangerine juice. Return to the stove and increase heat to high. Let sugar dissolve again, then add remaining tangerine juice. Reduce by one-third. Thicken slightly with arrowroot and strain.
5. Arrange duck slices on the plate and coat with citrus glaze.

Serves 8. Pair with a Long Island Cabernet Franc or Pinot Noir.

PECONIC BAY WINERY

HE FIRST VINES AT PECONIC BAY WINERY WERE PLANTED IN 1979 BY THE LATE LONG ISLAND WINE PIONEER RAY BLUM, MAKING THEM among the most mature on the East End. This property was the site of a circa-1900 farm, and the Dutch-style barn became Peconic Bay Winery's tasting house.

Recently renovated inside and out, the tasting house is an appealing mix of old and new. The updated green-trimmed exterior and a large, awning-sheltered patio set off by fresh landscaping beckon guests to enter the completely remodeled, light-filled tasting room, with its sleek, modern lines and long, spacious tasting bar.

Owners Paul and Ursula Lowerre both have busy careers in New York City and travel a lot, so they leave the management of Peconic Bay Winery, which they purchased in 1999, in the capable hands of Matt Gillies, a Long Island wine-industry veteran who started out as a teenager in 1979, toiling among the vines at Hargrave Vineyard. For a while he lived and worked with Kip Bedell, founder of Bedell Cellars. Over the years, Matt has planted and managed many East End vineyards. Under his watch at Peconic Bay, Gregory Gove was hired as winemaker and Charlie Hargrave as vineyard manager.

The Winemaker, Greg Gove
The February sky spits a cold drizzle as Matt Gillies walks a visitor down a brick path and across a gravel drive to Peconic Bay's winery, a converted barn painted a dusty shade of red. Inside, Greg Gove rises from behind his utilitarian metal desk in a corner of the winery, an arm's length from tall tanks of fermenting wine. Stepping over a hose snaking across the cement floor, the visitor takes a seat in the proffered rolling desk chair and asks Greg how he got started as a winemaker.

"I was a chemist for Columbia University," he begins. "I went to college for chemistry, and then I took some graduate courses at Columbia while working as a chemist there. It was kind of interesting stuff, environmental chemistry. They were trying to basically trace carbon dioxide as it traveled in the oceans and upwelling regions. You know, it affects fishing, it affects weather. . . . It was a lot of fun. It was a great job, a lot of traveling—South Africa, South America, out to sea and stuff.

"But if I wanted a real job and wanted to be able to pay rent," he says with a wry smile, "I'd have to get out of academia. I sort of came out here on a lark. I heard there were wineries out here; in 1985 there were only six. I started working at Hargrave, and I really liked it out here, partly because I like to sail."

Greg, who came to the North Fork from the Hudson Valley, worked at Hargrave Vineyard for about three years, until he felt he had learned all he could there. "I wanted to expand my horizons, and

Pindar at the time was growing about a dozen, fifteen different grapes and making port and sparkling wines," Greg says. "I found that interesting, so I went and worked at Pindar for about nine years."

One of the things he liked best about Pindar was working with their consultant, world-renowned winemaker Dimitri Tchelistcheff. "I found that very interesting and learned from him," says Greg. "And then I had an opportunity, in 1997, to actually use everything I'd learned and start up a winery."

That winery was Laurel Lake Vineyards, founded by Mike McGoldrick. "He had a building outlined and that was it," Greg recounts. "At one point I was taking care of the vineyards, making the wine, and looking after the tasting room, because Mike was all over the place. Sometimes I'd be in the winery, up on a ladder, and look out the window into the tasting room: 'Uh oh, there's people coming in!' And I'd scamper down and go over. But it was fun; I liked it."

In 1999 Greg's daughter was born and, since Laurel Lake Vineyards was up for sale, "I thought maybe I'd take a summer off and hang out with my daughter," he says. "My wife was working, and so I started doing that, but I still wanted to stay in the loop." He worked part-time at Peconic Bay and also at Pellegrini Vineyards, where he helped vineyard manager Charles Flatt plant a vineyard on Peconic Lane. "It was interesting to learn that aspect of it, with the laser-guided equipment and electronic drip irrigation and all that," Greg says.

Peconic Bay Winery wanted him full-time, but in light of his experience at Laurel Lake—the owner sold the business after Greg had invested so much of himself in it—he hesitated. "I didn't want to jump out of the frying pan into the fire. I wanted to make sure that the Lowerres were committed," he says.

Once he was convinced of the owners' staying power, Greg came on board at Peconic Bay. "It's a really nice setup for me personally," he says, "because Matt's been in business a while; Charlie Hargrave came on in 2001. I've known both of them for a long time, and there's no big egos here. We all have our own little spheres and we all get along; there's no bickering, no problems.

"Paul and Ursula Lowerre, they just want to make a good wine, so if I need something that will make better wine, or, more importantly, if Charlie needs something in the vineyard, he gets it," Greg says. "You can't make a nice wine out of mediocre grapes. I mean, there's no cutting corners: That's

it, period. That's nice. But then, on the other hand, there's also the burden on me, because Paul trusts me so much that it's important that I do what I can to save him money where I can, so I try to do that."

Peconic Bay Winery has grown substantially since Greg became the winemaker in 1999. "I've added one, two, three, four, tanks; that's about a thousand gallons," he says. "We've added ten acres of Chardonnay and about twenty acres of Merlot. We've expanded quite a bit on what Ray Blum had."

Back in 1998, Greg relates, the Lowerres had purchased 147 acres on Oregon Road in Mattituck; thirty acres of that have since been planted. "If you look at a map, that little section on the Sound is Oregon Hills, so we have a Merlot we call Oregon Hills Merlot."

Leaning back in his chair, Greg says, "I enjoy what I do. It's a bizarre job. A lot of people think of winemaking like you're sword fighting with a glass in your hand by candlelight, some romantic thing on the top of the tank, but if they saw what I do . . ." His voice trails off and he shakes his head in amusement. "I spend more time on ladders than roofers do—up and down and up and down. And you're always cleaning. You're doing most of your tasting in the morning, when your palate's fresh, and you're spitting, and you get in that habit.

"It's just a constant process of nurturing the wine," he continues. "You don't want to have to mess with it too much, you just want to sort of guide it, but it's a different kind of process than people think. You do have to be very mentally organized, I think."

Later, describing the miles of bureaucratic red tape wineries have to untangle, Greg says, "You wouldn't believe the regulations—the size of the numbers on your tanks! They want you to keep CO_2 records for your CO_2 tanks, because you could actually artificially increase the volume of a tank of wine by bubbling in CO_2. So they've got all their little rules, and I keep detailed records going back years. Every little thing I do, I keep track of the process and the gallons, and every few weeks I have to fill out forms."

He pulls out a file drawer stuffed full of government forms, takes one out, and shows his guest column upon column of tiny numbers. "A lot of people don't realize how strictly regulated we are," Greg says. "We have to keep track of every little thing. I guess some people think, well, you grow it on the vines, and you bring it in, and you just throw out bottles to people driving by!"

A moment later, with a touch of amazement in his voice, Greg says, "But somehow, even with all this regulation, you manage to make wine."

When his guest points out that he obviously manages to enjoy it, too, Greg replies, "Yeah, well, if you ask a lot of winemakers, they drink more beer than wine. Wine is work. Beer is more mindless, drinking without thinking. But quality beers. You won't find many winemakers who drink Bud and Coors Light.

"Wine, to winemakers, is work, and winemakers have a different slant on wine than wine writers," Greg goes on. "Wine writers, I've noticed, tend to look for positive attributes and something to be eloquent about. Winemakers are critical. We spend most of our time looking for the slightest defect or something that could be improved, and so you're always critical. If you see a bunch of winemakers sitting around tasting wines, they're looking for flaws. If you don't find flaws, then, 'Okay, this is a passable wine,' and then you go from there, on the quality of the tannins, the fruit, the acid balance and all that."

Asked if he's always in that critical mode while tasting wine, Greg responds, "Yeah, unless I'm at a dinner party with a lot of people; if you're, like, distracted and you're not thinking too much. But generally, if you're alone and there's no distractions, you're in that mode of being critical."

Greg muses aloud about what it's like to be a winemaker: "It's hard to imagine, but it's almost like raising a child. You start with the grapes, and you watch the evolution of that wine all the way to the bottle, and you see how it changes. And when it does everything you wanted it to do, you feel very proud that the wine has evolved in the way you assumed it would with only a little nudging here and there. So if there's some careless, crass wine writer that just dismisses it, it's like, 'Don't say anything about my kid! I know where you live!'"

The Wines

"We're sticking to our philosophy of making food-friendly wines: high quality, low volume, no expense spared," Greg says. Then he tells a story that clearly delights him: "Paul and Ursula are both very well traveled," he says. "They spend a lot of time in Europe, so he's pretty experienced with the wines of the world, and he knows a lot of experienced people.

"There was a guy who loved the wines from Mâcon," Greg continues, speaking of the white wine–producing area in the Burgundy region of France. When the Lowerres revealed that the wine they were sharing with him was not a Mâcon, Greg relates with gleeful pride, "He thought, 'Holy cow! I thought that's what I was drinking!' It was our steel Chardonnay!"

Peconic Bay's wines consistently win top awards and accolades.

La Barrique, its oaked Chardonnay, has won Best Oaked Chardonnay three times at the New York Wine and Food Classic. The 2005 vintage was named Best Wine Discovery (White) at the 2007 Wine Literary Awards in California, and it won a silver medal at the 2008 Tasters Guild International Wine Competition.

To mention just a few other awards in recent years: The 2005 Cabernet Franc, 2002 Cabernet Sauvignon, and 2001 Merlot Oregon Hills Reserve all won silver medals at the Tasters Guild competition; the Riesling was voted one of the top ten Rieslings in the United States at the Canberra International Riesling Challenge; at the New York Wine and Food Classic, the Merlot was chosen Best Merlot in New York State; the Florida State Fair competition awarded silver medals to the 2005 Steel-Fermented Chardonnay and 2005 Cabernet Franc; and the 2005 Riesling and Cabernet Franc also won silver at the Finger Lakes International Wine Competition.

Rounding out the current wine list are the 2006 Rosé of Merlot, Polaris Dessert Wine, and three easy-drinking, nonvintage table wines: Local Flavor Merlot, Local Flavor Red, and Local Flavor White.

Peconic Bay Winery
31320 Main Road, Cutchogue
(631) 734-7361
info@peconicbaywinery.com
www.peconicbaywinery.com
Open year-round
Owners: Ursula and Paul Lowerre
Winemaker: Greg Gove
Founded: 1979
Acres planted: 200
Varieties grown: Chardonnay, Cabernet Franc, Cabernet Sauvignon, Riesling, Merlot
Long Island Wine Council member

Waters Crest Winery

ATERS CREST WINERY HOLDS THE DISTINCTION OF BEING THE ONLY WINERY ON LONG ISLAND—AND PERHAPS IN the world—located in an industrial mall. But what it lacks in pastoral ambience it makes up for in the charm of its bistrolike tasting room, the warmth of its owners, and the quality of its wines.

"To me it's like a little oasis," says proprietor Linda Waters, "a place where you can go and relax and enjoy, spend a little time and get away from the crowd."

Indeed, visitors here are made to feel like welcome guests. If time allows, they might be treated to a personal tour of the compact but complete winery glimpsed through the big window behind the tasting counter.

"We bring people in the back because they have questions," says Linda's husband, Jim. "They get a lot of their questions answered, and that makes them feel connected."

That sense of connection is one of the things that makes Waters Crest such a pleasant place to visit.

The Owners, Jim and Linda Waters

Many East End winery owners made significant transitions between their former and current lives, but the change in Jim Waters's life—from living in

Linda and Jim Waters at the annual Merlot Classic, held at the Lenz Winery.

suburban Manorville, managing the Northeastern truck division for a big transportation company, and making wine in his spare time to living on the North Fork and running a winery—amounts to taking a flying leap across the Grand Canyon. It was a dramatic change, and it took a dramatic event to convince Jim and Linda the time had come to take that leap.

But even before that deciding moment, there were clear indications that a change was needed. "I had a very good job," says Jim, "but I was away from home, doing a lot of hours." One day he rushed home so Linda could leave for her job as an air traffic controller. "My little one was very upset," he says. "She was beside herself crying. And Linda just looked at me and said, 'You're not here. You're

just a guy that comes and goes.' And it really stuck with me. I hated that that job was the only way I felt I could get by."

Then came September 11, 2001. Jim, a volunteer firefighter with the Manorville Fire Department, was among the first responders at Ground Zero. "That was the turning point," Jim says. "I came home and said, 'You really live life one time.' " So he went from award-winning amateur winemaker to award-winning professional in one brave plunge.

Linda was behind her husband all the way. "After working all day," she says, "he'd come home and put his little boots on and make his wine, and he'd be singing. And I'm thinking, he's got to put that energy into a full-time thing. If you take that passion, that energy, that thing he loves to do—I

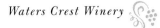

mean you obviously love to do it if you spend all your nights doing it—then I think it's going to be the right move. That's what I saw in him, and I said, you know what? It's the right thing to do, because you have to follow your passion."

"If I fail, then I know I tried, and I did the best I could," says Jim, and Linda adds, "But it's once in a lifetime, you know."

When they made the big move, there was no question where they were headed. "When we'd come out here to the North Fork, we'd always feel connected," Linda says. "I do commute; you still have to make the sacrifice, but there's the other sacrifice, for making life enjoyable."

One of the best changes for Jim is spending more time with his children. "On days like this, when my daughters play sports, I can leave and go see them," he says with evident pleasure.

"The way we look at it," he adds, "we can make a living, we can take our trip a year, we can do other things—that's all we're looking for in life; we're not looking for a lot. And we like what we do. For me, I work a lot of hours, and I work hard and I'm involved in everything. But I like what I'm doing, and my days go by very full. I feel like I get a lot out of it."

There's no doubt about Jim's love of wine-making. Leaning forward in his chair as his deep voice booms out, he tells a guest, "Wherever we go, we always have to find the wine country. We always take one day and we go, 'Okay, where's the winery?' And we'll get in the car and go. We've been doing that our whole life. And every time I walked into a winery there was that smell, the smell of a winery—as soon as you walk in, you just go, 'Ahh.' You know that's what you're supposed to do."

And they knew where they were meant to be. "Here, you know where you belong," Linda says. "I

think all your life you follow your passion to where you're supposed to be."

The Wines

"Making wine isn't about chemistry, yet it is," says Jim. "You nurture it, you create its direction. So when you're very passionate about it and you feel everything—the way it tastes, the way you rack it, and

Linda Waters with Long Island Wine Ambassadors Rich and Chris Gordon.

the way you handle it, the way you harvest the berries . . . It's everything you do, and I can't describe it, but me and Linda know it because we're connected to every bottle."

When visitors ask Jim what his best wine is, he tells them, "I don't have a best wine. It's every wine that I make. I put a lot of passion in every wine, and I say, 'At certain times of the year, I love rosé, I love Chardonnay, I love reds.' I put my passion in everything I make."

"That's what he does," Linda says. "It's part of him."

"That's right, exactly," Jim confirms. "There's no formula. I think the fruit and the direction of the wine, it talks to us and tells us what it wants to do. People say to me, 'Oh, the '03 had this.' It's not Budweiser! Every year is different based on what's in the vineyard."

Jim gets his fruit from top North Fork growers, picking out certain blocks and even individual rows in the vineyard. His passion and meticulous care in the winery have produced many award winners, including double gold and Best White Vinifera Blend in the 2006 International Eastern Wine Competition for his intense and luscious dessert wine, Night Watch.

Waters Crest produces Rosé, Chardonnay, Merlot, Cabernet Franc, a Mediterranean-style red blend called Campania Rossa, and limited bottlings of Riesling and Gewürztraminer. From the best vintages Jim makes a Meritage Bordeaux blend and reserve versions of other reds and whites. All of his wines have won medals and high ratings in nearly every vintage.

This small winery produces only a few thousand cases each year and sells out quickly. Certain special bottlings are available only to wine club members.

Waters Crest Winery
Route 48 and Cox Lane, Cutchogue
(631) 734-5065
jwaters0@optonline.net
www.waterscrestwinery.com
Open year-round
Owners: Jim and Linda Waters
Winemaker: Jim Waters
Founded: 2002
Grapes purchased from various Long Island vineyards
Long Island Wine Council member

PUGLIESE VINEYARDS

UGLIESE VINEYARDS IS ONE OF THOSE SPOTS THAT'S HIDDEN FROM THE ROAD, BUT WHEN YOU DRIVE IN, YOU FIND A DELIGHTFUL SURPRISE. A long arbor draped with grapevines and a pond with a fountain at its center make this place especially welcoming, and the ancient red gas pump on the lawn adds just the right touch of rustic whimsy.

Inside the tasting room, you're almost certain to be greeted by a member of the Pugliese family behind the bar. It might be Pat herself, who is there seven days a week. It might be her daughter, Domenica, or a daughter-in-law, or a nephew. In the summer, when it's really busy, a few close friends help out, too.

Ralph Sr., the patriarch, founded the family business and keeps his hand in. Peter, the middle son, makes the wine. Lawrence, the youngest, manages the vineyard. Ralph Jr., the eldest, a talented landscape photographer, helps out when he's needed.

Co-owner, Patricia Pugliese
On a weekday well before the start of the busy season, Pat Pugliese talks with a visitor about the founding of her family's vineyard and winery in the early 1980s.

"My husband was retired," Pat begins, "and I was just a domestic engineer and whatever-have-you. We were looking for a little summer home, so we came out to Cutchogue and found a tiny cottage with two acres that we decided to purchase for a getaway in the summertime, for the children, to bring them from the city to the country.

"We had two acres of land, and we put a few tomato plants in and whatever-have-you," she continues. "And then the farmer that lived next door to me told me that he had ten acres of property adjoining our two acres, and if we wanted to purchase it, he was going to give us the first option on it, which we decided to purchase. And with that, we put in two acres of grapevines the following year."

At that time the Puglieses had no intention of entering the wine business, Pat says. "We were going to take the grapes home that we produced and make wine, because my husband always made wine back in the city." But they ended up with too many grapes to transport, so they began selling them to Pindar, and in the fourth year they started making wine for sale in the basement of their Cutchogue home.

When the operation outgrew the basement, they moved it to the garage. "And then, when it got to be too much, we decided to put a big building just back there," she says, indicating the land behind the tasting house. "We put a building there; we have a Champagne cellar there; we have all the wine tanks there, the wine storage, and that's it."

Since that modest beginning Pugliese Vineyards has grown to encompass more than fifty acres of vines. Pat admits the family didn't realize how much work it was going to be.

"It was rough, because when we first started, we had no money for machinery or equipment," she says. "We were putting all the grapevines in the ground by hand. My sons used a post-digger. We put in each vine individually and covered them up, and I think the following year we put the posts in, and then the wire, and we bought a secondhand tractor, used barrels, used stainless-steel tanks. And then it gets big. It starts to grow when you need this, and you need so many different things."

In those early days most new vineyard owners learned what worked the hard way, by trial and error. One of the hard lessons the Puglieses learned was that the shape of vineyard posts is all-important.

Ralph Sr. made all his posts by hand, out of cement. "The big mistake on that," Pat says, "was he made them square; he didn't round them out like a pole is rounded out, where the wind will go around it. So when we had Hurricane Gloria, she knocked all

the cement posts down. They cracked and broke; we had to get rid of them and buy the wooden posts."

The Puglieses have learned a great deal since then, but running a vineyard, winery, and tasting room doesn't get any easier. "It's a seven-day-a-week job, and it's 365 days a year just in the vineyard, the preparation of the vineyard itself, because that's the key to making wine: the vineyard," Pat says. "You need someone there to prune; you need someone there to do the harvest, to do the spray program, get rid of the weeds and whatever-have-you."

One of Pat's special tasks and talents is painting some of the wine bottles. "I painted in oils before we had the winery," Pat tells her guest, "and then, when we opened up the winery, we decided to make Champagne, and I was looking for a special label for my Champagne bottles. So I got a lot of different paints out, and pens and whatever-have-you, and I just started to write on the bottles, and I came up with the design. I liked it so much I had all my wines packaged with the same labels—paper labels—but the Champagne bottles are hand-painted and a few odds-and-ends bottles are hand-painted."

Each bottle takes about twenty-five minutes to paint, she says. "My first bottle that we released with the hand-painting was 1988. And we won a few awards for the label at the San Diego International Wine Competition."

Pat's beautifully painted bottles and glasses are popular with Pugliese's customers, but she's much more proud of her son Peter's skill at winemaking. "Peter wins a lot of medals every year in competitions," she says. "He won the biggest award in California—Los Angeles, I believe it was. He won for Champagne, the Best in Show, and he won two gold medals with the same bottle of Champagne." Pointing toward the front of the tasting room, Pat

says, "That big silver platter, and the picture frame with the grapes on it—I've got my son's picture in there."

The Winemaker, Peter Pugliese

Peter has been in the wine business for most of his life. "I was ten years old, and my dad and my mom would take the four siblings out here from Queens," he recalls. "And then we planted two acres of Chardonnay in 1980. I always worked with my brother, and from there it just grew. Each year we planted a few more acres, and a few more acres, until last year we just about finished the rest of our fields. We have about fifty-three acres planted."

Asked to describe his journey from young boy helping out in the vineyard to winemaker, Peter says,

"I used to work with my dad when our production was a lot smaller. The first year was 1986. We made—I think it was about three hundred cases of Chardonnay. We had just a few barrels at the time. And over each year, until about '90, when I moved out here permanently, I kind of took over with the winemaking. My dad taught me, and there were some other winemakers on the island; if I needed any help with something, I went to them. And we also had an enologist who would come in the fall, right before we started picking the grapes for harvest, and he taught me quite a few techniques to make a better wine every year. This my seventeenth full year I'm actually making the wine."

Not only does Peter make the wine, but he also helps out in other areas of the business. "It's a family operation, so if I'm needed in the tasting room when the warm weather comes—from Memorial Day weekend all the way until Christmas—I'm working here on the weekends, and I also do the weed spraying."

Peter's grandfather immigrated to the United States from Naples, Italy, and brought the family's winemaking tradition with him. "They always did home winemaking in Queens and Brooklyn," Peter says, "his brother and his brother-in-law. They used to make about three hundred gallons a year. In 1986 our first commercial vintage was only five hundred gallons, so it wasn't really that much more. But this fall we had most of the rest of our new Merlot field come in, and we were up to about ten thousand cases. This year we're up to about thirteen thousand cases," he says.

As for his winemaking philosophy, Peter says it's pretty simple: "It's just like everyone is realizing, which is that the best fruit that you can grow makes a wine very easy to make. If you're dealing with fruit that's underripe, or if you have some rot in there, obviously the quality isn't going to be as high. So we just try to have the vineyard maintained to the highest quality, and it will produce a great wine, hopefully."

The Wines
Pugliese Vineyards wines have earned many awards over the years in such prestigious competitions as the Tasters Guild, Finger Lakes International Wine Competition, International Eastern Wine Competition, and San Diego National Wine Competition. Most recently as of this writing, the 2005 Raffaello White Port won a bronze medal in the 2007 New York Wine and Food Classic.

Pugliese's current wine list offers more than twenty wines. White varietals include Reserve and Gold-label Chardonnay, Pinot Grigio, Riesling, and Gewürztraminer. Reds varietals include Sangiovese, Cabernet Franc, Cabernet Sauvignon Reserve, and Merlot Reserve. Currently offered blends and specialty wines include white, blush, and red table wines called, respectively, Bella Francesca, Bella Maria, and Bella Domenica; Sunset Meritage; Late Harvest Riesling; Late Harvest Gewürztraminer; Late Harvest Niagara; Raffaello White Port; and Porto Bello in two vintages, 2001 and 1998. Several sparkling wines are offered: Blanc de Noir (Nature), Blanc de Blanc Brut, Sparkling Merlot, and Dolce Patricia.

Pugliese Vineyards
Main Road, Cutchogue
(631) 734-4057
pugliesewines@pugliesevineyards.com
www.pugliesevineyards.com
Open year-round
Owners: Patricia and Ralph Pugliese
Winemaker: Peter Pugliese
Founded: 1980
Acres planted: 53
Varieties grown: Chardonnay, Niagara, Gewürztraminer, Pinot Grigio, Riesling, Cabernet Franc, Cabernet Sauvignon, Merlot, Pinot Noir, Sangiovese, Syrah
Long Island Wine Council member

BEDELL CELLARS

BEDELL CELLARS' TRADITIONAL EXTERIOR MAKES ITS GLEAMING, BLACK AND WHITE AND CHROME TASTING ROOM AN EYE-OPENING SURPRISE. Outside, the grounds are lushly landscaped, inviting leisurely walks, and the clean lines of the cupola-topped, barn-style buildings hint of the sophistication within. A covered pavilion with a tasting bar extends into an open deck that overlooks acres of vines marching in neat rows to the distant tree line.

Something special here is owner Michael Lynne's art collection. Works by such renowned contemporary artists as Cindy Sherman, Uta Barth, Sam Taylor Wood, Eric Fischl, Ross Bleckner, Barbara Kruger, Sarah Morris, Howard Shatz, and Chuck Close adorn the walls, and some of the same artwork appears on the wine labels.

Bedell Cellars was founded in 1980 by Kip Bedell. Two decades later, although he had no plans to sell, he was presented with a very attractive offer by Michael Lynne, co-chairman and co-CEO of New Line Cinema and executive producer the *Lord of the Rings* trilogy and many other outstanding successes. Michael became the new owner of Bedell Cellars in 2000.

An enthusiastic art collector, Michael has also been building his collection of fine wines for many years. Eventually his interest in wine led to a desire to own a vineyard. After searching in California, Italy, and France, he visited the North Fork and happened to meet Kip. Impressed with the quality of the wine he found in the region, and particularly at Bedell Cellars, he decided this was the winery for him.

Under Michael's ownership substantial renovation and expansion have taken place, including the purchase of brand-new, state-of-the-art equipment from Italy, France, and Germany.

The reorganized business also brought in Pascal Marty as consulting enologist. Educated in Bordeaux in his home country of France, Pascal spent fourteen years as director of winemaking for the legendary Baron Philippe de Rothschild. While still at Rothschild, Pascal oversaw a joint venture with Robert Mondavi Winery in California that produced Opus One, the famous Bordeaux blend that in 1984 started the trend toward ultra-premium wines. In 1997 he developed the first Chilean super-premium wine, Viña Almaviva, for the huge wine company Concha y Toro. Such top wine critics as Robert Parker and *Wine Spectator* consistently give Pascal's wines scores ranging from 95 to 100.

The Chief Operating Officer, Trent Preszler

Another key hire was Trent Preszler. Trent managed the expansion, recruited the winemaking team, increased international brand recognition, and launched the Artist Series wine labels. His efforts were instrumental in Bedell Cellars being named one of the 2006 ten Hottest Small Brands in America by *Wine Business Monthly*.

Raised on a South Dakota cattle ranch, Trent turned an interest in botany into a master's degree in that subject; he earned another advanced degree in agricultural economics at Cornell University in upstate New York.

"The first time I became aware of Long Island wine was probably in 2000, when I began work on my master's thesis at Cornell," Trent says. "I tasted a few wines at that time but didn't have a very in-depth knowledge of the region. It wasn't until Michael Lynne brought me here that I really became immersed.

"The region has definitely changed since then," he continues. "The wine quality and level of excellence have risen to new heights, and I think a lot of wineries are seeing the results."

Trent returned to Cornell in 2008 to pursue a PhD in viticulture. He maintains an advisory role at the winery.

The Founding Winemaker, Kip Bedell

In 1970, when his brother gave him his first home winemaking kit, Kip Bedell was living in Garden City and running his fuel oil business in West Hempstead. "That first wine was awful, undrinkable," Kip admits. "I took it as a challenge and tried again." But the path that led him from that point to planting a vineyard was long and unexpected.

Unlike many "up-islanders," Kip knew the North Fork well. "My grandparents had a house in Mattituck. I have many fond memories of coming out with my cousins in the summer, playing on the beach."

He was still coming out to the North Fork with his wife, Susan, when the Hargraves planted their vineyard in 1973. "We were very interested in what they were doing," says Kip. "We came out and helped pick and talked. We thought maybe someday we'd start something like that."

Within a few years several other people had gotten involved in the nascent industry, and Kip and

Susan decided to join them. "We started looking for land in 1977," Kip says, "thinking of maybe three or four acres. I'm not quite sure how we ended up with fifty!" They found the Cutchogue property in 1979 and put in seven acres of vines in 1980. They sold their first vintage in 1986, from a picnic table set up in the 1919 potato barn that served as winery, tasting room, tractor shed, and maintenance garage.

For the first ten years, they drove out on weekends, staying with their two young sons in the property's old farmhouse. Then, in 1990, they sold the fuel oil business, bought a newer house in Cutchogue, and moved to the North Fork.

During the years leading up to the change in ownership, Kip earned a reputation for crafting exceptional reds, so much so that he was often referred to as "Mr. Merlot," a moniker he still hears from time to time. Although his time at the winery is now limited to three days a week, he's still very much immersed in the business he loves.

"I've always been an amateur artist," says Kip, "and there's a lot of artistic involvement in winemaking. So many decisions are scientific, but also artistic. It's up to you to sculpt the wine so you'll enjoy it yourself and other people will enjoy it and buy it. It's still fascinating. I still love to do it."

Kip admits to feeling sentimental about selling the winery. But his two sons weren't interested in taking over, and Michael made him an offer that proved irresistible. "Michael promised me his goal was to make the best wine he could," Kip recounts, "and he's been as good as his word."

Back in 1980, Kip admits, he could never have imagined what the future would bring. "We were a small band," he recalls: "the Hargraves, Ray Blum, Dr. Dan [Damianos], Peter Lenz. . . . I don't think any of us had a clue. There was the sense that grapes grew here, but no sense that we could make great wine."

The Winemaker, Kelly Urbanik

Although the number of female winemakers is growing rapidly, in 2008 there were only two on the East End. As one of those two (the other is Macari Vineyards' flying winemaker Paola Valverde), Kelly Urbanik has earned bragging rights. But this talented young Californian, whose straight hair is pulled back in a casual ponytail, exudes forthright good humor and modesty.

A visitor asks Kelly about her journey from northern California to Long Island. "I grew up in St. Helena in Napa Valley," she begins, "and so I grew up around wine. My grandpa had a vineyard. It wasn't a vineyard where he was selling the fruit; it was a very small vineyard. It was always something that we just did for fun, and that's where I kind of got interested in it."

Thinking she might go into viticulture, Kelly attended the University of California, Davis, where she chose a dual major in viticulture and enology with a minor in French. With characteristic modesty Kelly mentions that she went to France on a student exchange program. What she doesn't say is that she was given the opportunity because she was chosen as a Laureate by the prestigious Confrérie des Chevaliers du Tastevin (Brotherhood of Knights of Wine-Tasting Cups), an exclusive organization devoted to wines from the Burgundy region.

It was while working in the cellar at Maison Louis Jadot in 2003 that Kelly decided to concentrate on winemaking. "I like the winemaking part of it," she says. "I mean, you have to know a lot about the vineyard to even work with winemaking, but to me it felt right to be in the winery."

Winemaker Kelly Urbanik in her lab.

Back in California, Kelly got a job as assistant winemaker at Bouchaine Vineyards in the Carneros region in southern Napa Valley. "They grow mostly Pinot and Chardonnay, more like the Burgundy varietals," she says. "So I was working there and I was living in Napa, and it was like, 'OK, I've lived here most of my life.' I was kind of looking for a change of scenery, so I was starting to think about other places in California, and then this opportunity came at Bedell."

When she found out it was in New York, Kelly was dubious, to say the least. "But they sent me pictures of the winery and of the area, and it looked pretty nice. Then I came out here and checked it out, and it was like—it was awesome that this existed, so I was like, 'Wow!' I felt like if I didn't come here, I would have missed a really good opportunity."

When Kelly talks about Kip Bedell, her admiration is obvious. "Kip's pretty much my hero;

I tell everyone that," she declares. "Any question you have, he knows the answer, and he knows every little corner of this winery, which of course makes sense. He's the type of person I always wanted to work for."

Kelly is an enthusiastic defender of Long Island against the doubt any new wine region is bound to encounter. And as a former Napa winemaker, she's uniquely qualified to speak up when people attempt to compare the two regions.

"I feel like you can't compare them at all," she says. "It's totally different here, and I really feel Long Island can stand on its own. People are going to turn to Long Island because they're going to get awesome wines that aren't 16 percent alcohol, wines that are balanced. I think it's awesome that we can do that—have ripe fruit that still has acid and still has good flavors that aren't jammy or overripe."

Summing up her time at Bedell Cellars, Kelly says without hesitation, "I really, really like it here. I feel like it was the right choice for me."

The Wines

While continuing to produce distinctive varietals, Bedell Cellars is increasing its focus on blends. Kelly describes the philosophy at Bedell as "bringing the art into the wine, being creative and trying to make something unique."

As of this writing, the elegantly named Musée is the newest addition to Bedell Cellars' wine list. An ultra-premium Bordeaux blend aged fifteen months in French oak, Musée will be produced only from the best vines and vintages. "The reaction to this wine has been overwhelmingly positive, and it's on its way to being sold out," reports Trent Preszler. Highly respected wine critic Anthony Dias Blue gave Musée 90 points, an "outstanding" score. Contemporary artist Chuck Close of Bridgehampton designed the label, which features a daguerreotype of deep purple grapes.

Bedell also offers a much-praised ultra-premium white blend called Gallery, whose label was designed by artist Ross Bleckner.

The winery's Taste series has earned high praise, not only for the contents, but also for the label by Barbara Kruger. The word *taste* floats in the open mouth of a close-up of an iconic, Marilyn Monroe–like face. Taste Red and Taste White are artful blends of several varieties.

Bedell Cellars' handsome B label is reserved for estate-bottled wines sourced from its own North Fork vineyards. Currently in the tasting room are the B-label Reserve Merlot, Estate Merlot, Reserve Chardonnay, and Estate Chardonnay. Also new to the wine list in 2008 is a pair of easy-drinking table wines, First Crush Red and First Crush White.

Bedell Cellars
Main Road, Cutchogue
(631) 734-7537
winemail@bedellcellars.com
www.bedellcellars.com
Open year-round
Owner: Michael Lynne
Founding winemaker: Kip Bedell
Winemaker: Kelly Urbanik
Consulting enologist: Pascal Marty
Founded: 1980
Acres planted: 57
Varieties grown: Chardonnay, Riesling, Gewürztraminer, Viognier, Cabernet Franc, Cabernet Sauvignon, Merlot, Petit Verdot
Long Island Wine Council member

Oysters Baked in Garlic and Pernod

Chef John Ross

2 dozen oysters

1 head green kale

2 tablespoons olive oil

1 tablespoon minced garlic

¼ cup minced shallots

1 tablespoon Pernod

Coarse salt and pepper

4 tablespoons unsalted butter, melted

3 tablespoons panko (Japanese bread crumbs) or other coarse, dry bread crumbs

6 ounces thinly sliced pancetta (Italian bacon)

Lemon wedges

1. Shuck the oysters, reserving bottom shells. Place the rinsed shells on a sheet pan (bury them in rock salt if desired) and hold oyster meats in the refrigerator.
2. Wash the kale and remove ribs. Chop the leaves into 2-inch pieces and pat dry.
3. In a sauté pan heat olive oil and add garlic and shallots. Over high heat add the kale along with the Pernod and a little coarse salt and pepper. Cook about 3 minutes and remove from heat.
4. Preheat oven to 425°F. Place kale mixture in the bottom of the oyster shells and put the oyster meats on top. Spoon melted unsalted butter over oysters and sprinkle them with bread crumbs. Put a small piece of pancetta on each oyster and bake until oysters just begin to curl and crumbs begin to brown.
5. Remove oysters from oven and serve with lemon wedges.

Serves 4. Pair with a crisp Long Island Sauvignon Blanc or dry Riesling.

PINDAR VINEYARDS

THE VINEYARDS AT PINDAR STRETCH FROM THE MAIN ROAD TO THE NORTH ROAD. ITS NEARLY SEVEN HUNDRED ACRES OF VINES MAKE it the largest on Long Island. The architecture of the sprawling building that houses the tasting room is an interesting mix of classical and modern, with streamlined white columns in front and multilayered, red-tiled roof gables. Inside, the dark wood lends an Old World feeling to the large foyer. To your left a couple of steps lead to the tasting room, where long, U-shaped tasting bars accommodate large numbers of guests eager to try Pindar's wide variety of wines.

The most striking feature of the tasting room is a large, Tiffany-style stained-glass window. Out back is a spacious pavilion for relaxing and sipping on a warm summer's day. This is also the scene of live music and even the occasional opera.

A state-of-the-art winery was built several years ago to house new temperature-controlled stainless-steel tanks, catwalks, and a twenty-five-ton press. The climate-controlled barrel cellar holds three thousand barrels, and an automated riddling machine does the tedious job of periodically turning aging sparkling wine seven hundred bottles at a time.

The Owners, Dr. Herodotus Damianos and family

Dr. Herodotus Damianos, known as Dr. Dan, was a physician practicing internal medicine in Stony Brook when he decided to jump into eastern Long Island's fledgling wine industry. What drew him here were dual interests in wine and agriculture.

"My parents are of European origin, and they were certainly familiar with wine," Dr. Dan says. "That transcended in small part to the home in which I grew up in New York City. But I think it was just an interest in agriculture, mostly. I think if you live in a concrete jungle and then you see your first tomato, you're hooked. That's exactly what happened to me. We had a little backyard and my dad had planted some tomato plants, etc., and it was just fascinating to see these things grow, so I think that's where it began."

After Dr. Dan opened his medical practice in Stony Brook, his interest in agriculture was transferred to Long Island. He zeroed in on viticulture after members of a horticulture research institute visited the area. "When the Geneva Extension of Cornell University came down in 1968 or 1969 because of the problem of the golden nematode in potatoes, they said we had such a wonderful climate, that it was like Bordeaux and perhaps we could grow *vinifera* grapes here."

That sparked his interest even more. In 1979 he bought thirty-six acres of the former Krupski farm. With help from his two older sons, Alexander and Jason, he planted ten acres of Chardonnay in 1980. "I fully understood that farming was not an easy thing, but with the kind of work I did, it was a joy to get out in the fields and work," says Dr. Dan. "Being a physician is an awful lot of mental pressure, and physical exertion was a good tonic."

Dr. Dan made Pindar Vineyards' first wines with help from a UC Davis enology program graduate. Today Jason Damianos is head winemaker at Pindar (he also produces small quantities from his own Jason's Vineyard in Jamesport). Alexander runs the family's South Fork winery, Duck Walk.

Pindar, the youngest brother, has taken on the task of managing the vineyards. He talks about growing into his father's dream: "Working in the vineyard over the summers, I just kind of fell in love with it. Each of us has a different aspect of the business that we fell in love with as kids. Mine was the vineyard; Jason's was winemaking; Alexander's was the marketing. We just seem to fall into the different categories, and we work well together."

Jason and Pindar both graduated from the viticulture and enology program at California State University, Fresno, where Jason won a platinum medal for the wine he created, a blueberry port. Jason then spent two and a half years at the University of Bordeaux, continuing his education in enology. It was there he learned that planting the vines closer

together than was practiced on Long Island at the time would improve the quality of the grapes. When he returned home in 1996, Jason planted his own twenty-acre vineyard with European spacing. Now Pindar Vineyards is one of many on Long Island that has been interplanted with new vines.

After thirty years Dr. Dan's love for the family's vineyards is still evident. "To me it's always very exciting, and each new season is a new renaissance," he says. "I like it in the wintertime when it's cold and there's a light snow; the vineyards look beautifully stark—snow on the canes. They're all nicely pruned, and then in the spring we have bud break, and you see tiny little spots of green on the wood. I love to see that!

"And then it turns purple, little purple dots," Dr. Dan continues. "That, to me, is the prettiest time.

Then suddenly there's bud burst, and the buds open up and the leaves start coming out, and there's tremendous growth. And then it's summertime, a big canopy, and you see the small grapes beginning to form. They're green, and then they get bigger and start turning yellow and gold, and then it's August. I love that, because we go through the fields and pick our grapes and bring them in to press and crush them. Then in the fall, as the leaves gradually fall off the vines and you can see all of the canes before pruning, that's a different look, too. Then in the wintertime the pruning begins again, and then it cycles back again. It's always very exciting; you never get tired of that."

Pindar tells what it's like to be the one managing the vines: "It's exciting throughout the growing season, and it's challenging, but in September and

October all your hard work really pays off when you bring in the fruit. There are lows in vineyard management in the winter; it's very quiet and surreal out there. But I think harvest is best, because all your hard work is getting paid off. You leave your crop at the back door of the fermentation room and you don't really see it until the vintages start coming out, and you see your '07 or '05 Cab Franc, and your grapes are starting to win awards."

The Wines

Pindar Vineyards has always produced a long list of different styles of wines, from sweet and simple whites to complex and elegant Bordeaux-style blends.

Dr. Dan explains the reasoning behind this variety: "When we started, this was an entirely new, infant industry. Long Islanders in those days were not really wine drinkers, so it was very important to embark on a program of education. This is what we did successfully at Pindar, and we're continuing to do that by having frequent tours, explaining to people how vines grow, showing them the process of making wine, bringing them in to taste our wines.

"Most people who start drinking wine prefer semidry wines, which is fine," he continues. "After a while their palate becomes more educated and they gradually go to the drier wines, which is of course what we look for, because these are the wines that complement food. Our major philosophy is to produce wines that are food friendly."

Pindar Vineyards is probably best known for Mythology, a proprietary Bordeaux-style red blend that has won numerous top awards and rave reviews. Renowned wine critic Anthony Dias Blue named Mythology one of the top fifty wines of the world.

Beyond one or more tiers of Cabernet, Chardonnay, Merlot, and easy-drinking red and white blends, Pindar currently produces Gamay Beaujolais, Syrah, Viognier, Semillon, Riesling, Sauvignon Blanc, Port, and a dessert-dry Cuvée Rare made from 100 percent Pinot Meunier. Another award-winning red blend, Pythagoras, is a customer favorite. Every year Pindar wines win numerous awards at prestigious competitions.

Winemaking is never static at Pindar Vineyards. "We're always changing," says Jason. "We plant different varieties, try different things. In the last couple of years, we've come out with Late Harvest Sauvignon Blanc, Late Harvest Chardonnay, Semillon, and Semillon Blanc. And we're coming out with a new type of Champagne, Blanc de Blanc, which is 100 percent Chardonnay. We're always working toward the future, trying to make better wine."

Pindar Vineyards
Main Road, Peconic
(631) 734-6200
info@pindar.net
www.pindar.net
Open year-round
Owners: Dr. Herodotus Damianos and family
Winemaker: Jason Damianos
Founded: 1979
Acres planted: 667
Major varieties grown: Chardonnay, Gewürztraminer, Riesling, Sauvignon Blanc, Semillon, Viognier, Cabernet Sauvignon, Gamay Beaujolais, Merlot, Petit Verdot, Pinot Meunier, Syrah
Long Island Wine Council member

THE LENZ WINERY

HE LENZ WINERY IS APPROACHED BY A BREEZEWAY THROUGH THE MIDDLE OF A MANSARD-ROOFED STRUCTURE WHOSE shallow steps are flanked by wine barrels topped with potted plants. On the other side of this portal, you glimpse the trunk of a huge tree; beyond it, a wall of green. A few steps and you emerge into a courtyard with the ambience of a winery in the French countryside.

To your right, beyond an arbor thick with flowers, is a restored farmhouse, legacy of a time when most of the wineries were barns set behind farmhouses facing the Main Road. To your left is the tasting room, its porch shaded by a dense canopy of grapevines that snake up, thicker than a man's arm, next to the wooden support posts. The tasting room is a rustic beauty, but the vineyard and winemaking practices here are far from rustic.

Lenz was founded in 1978 and has some of the oldest vines on Long Island. Vineyard manager Sam McCullough employs all the tools at his command, including leaf removal, shoot and cluster thinning, crop reduction, and meticulous pest and fungus control, to bring in healthy, optimally ripe fruit.

The Owner, Peter Carroll

Peter Carroll, co-owner of Lenz with his wife, Deborah, exudes a boyish charm complemented by his wry British sense of humor and easy laugh, often at his own expense. Peter grew up in the English countryside, took an engineering degree at Cambridge, and then went to business school. He was hired by Chase Bank in New York City in 1974. Soon he struck out on his own, starting a management consulting business. With his background, Peter says he's never afraid to ask how something works.

He met Deborah in the Hamptons. Back then, in 1982, neither of them knew about the nascent wine region just across the Great Peconic Bay. But they heard about a windsurfing regatta held on the North Fork and, being into water sports, they investigated.

"We would drive over to the North Fork in our little Audi coupe, and there would be this fabulous regatta in Mattituck," Peter recounts. "We thought, 'Wow, this is really neat!' So we started coming over to the North Fork and renting a little cottage in New Suffolk, and then we noticed that all these vineyards were there."

Intrigued, Peter did what he's trained to do: analyze. "I took a pad of paper and a pencil, and I started thinking, 'I wonder how much an acre of land costs. I wonder how many vines you can put on an acre. I wonder how many pounds of grapes you get off each vine. I wonder how many gallons of wine you get. I wonder how much you sell the wine for. I wonder how much the bottles cost.' I ran through all the numbers, and I don't have those scribblings,

but if I did they would be hilarious, because they all turned out to be completely incorrect!" His laughter rings through the courtyard.

With encouragement from a business friend and advice from young vineyard manager Matt Gillies, Peter decided to go for it. He sold his house in Westhampton, bought farmland on Oregon Road in Mattituck, and planted twenty acres of Chardonnay and ten acres of Cabernet Sauvignon.

They were planning to convert a barn on that property into a winery, but then Peter heard that Lenz was up for sale. By September 1988 Peter and Debbie were the new owners of the Lenz Winery.

"Growing grapes is an extremely practical business," Peter says. "You have to plant the vines, treat them right, prune them, spray them, pick them. There's a lot of dimension to the process of making good wine. Conceptually, it's pretty straightforward, but it involves a very challenging set of trade-offs, which I enjoy.

"It's a bit like I enjoy sailing," he explains. "I don't really enjoy just sailing around the bay; I enjoy racing. When you're racing you have to set everything right, because you want to be doing better than the other boats. So you've got to adjust the mainsheet, the downhaul, the outhaul—and then the conditions change, and you're always tinkering.

"Growing grapes is a bit like that," Peter says, concluding his analogy. "There are a lot of controls you can play with to get the kind of grapes that will make really good wine."

The Winemaker, Eric Fry

Like many winemakers, Eric Fry arrived on the East End by a circuitous route. After graduating from Indiana State University with degrees in microbiology and psychology—"I understand how

Winemaker Eric Fry

bacteria think," he jokes—he headed to the University of California, Davis, to offer his services to an elderly geneticist there whom he greatly admired. But by the time he arrived, his would-be mentor had died of old age. Eric was staying with friends in Calistoga in Napa Valley, so, even though he had no experience in the wine industry, he decided to make the rounds of the wineries.

"The first winery I walked into was Mondavi," Eric recounts. "I said, 'I'm a microbiologist. I have no idea if you guys need one, but I'd like to apply for a job.'" A few minutes later, Zelma Long, Mondavi's renowned winemaker, came downstairs and told Eric, "I want to talk to you!" The vines at Mondavi had been infested with the flavor-spoiling yeast

Brettanomyces, and the board had decided to hire a microbiologist just a day or two before Eric showed up looking for a job.

Eric was in charge of the analysis lab at Mondavi, overseeing as many as fourteen chemists at harvest time. "In my 'old age' now, as a winemaker," he says, "I don't do chemistry anymore. I taste the wine and make all my decisions.

"Science is important," he continues, "because you can screw up big time if you don't pay attention to what's going on, but it's not a numbers thing. Mondavi was corporate, so they wanted numbers on everything. We're not corporate here, so if I taste the wine and I have a picture in my brain of that wine, that's all that matters."

While he was with Mondavi, Eric worked in western Australia; then he left Mondavi and went to France, working in Provence and Cognac. Back in the United States, he landed at Jordan Winery in Napa Valley, where he met famed enologist André Tchelistcheff. By that time Eric knew he wanted to make his own wine, and he asked the legendary winemaker's advice.

"He sent me to Dr. Frank," Eric says, referring to Konstantin Frank, a pioneering vintner in New York's Finger Lakes region. "I was skeptical, but I went to talk to Dr. Frank, and I saw the vineyards were gorgeous, in spite of the fact that they were in the Finger Lakes, which, coming from California, was not a good thing. But the grapes were incredibly beautiful, so I said, 'Okay, fine.' I was at Dr. Frank's for three or four years, and then I got a call from Peter, and I came down here and talked to him, and I've been here ever since."

The Lenz Winery

Eric prowls the vineyard as harvest approaches, tasting a grape here, a grape there, until they are perfect for the wine he has in mind. He might want some Chardonnay picked before it's fully ripe to maintain bright citrus and pineapple flavors. A week or so later, when softer characteristics of pear and apple appear, more Chardonnay will be brought in. The last clusters might hang until they're extremely ripe to build up sweetness and add complexity to the wine. When the grapes taste exactly right, Eric says, "Pick!" and the harvest begins.

A self-proclaimed "control freak" in the vineyard, Eric is the opposite in the cellar. He's well aware of all the chemical tricks available but believes in letting the wine do its own thing as much as possible. He tastes tirelessly, blends judiciously, and waits, more or less patiently, for the natural chemistry that has been turning grape juice into wine since long before human beings discovered the delights of the beverage.

The Wines

On a warm, overcast summer day, a guest stands in a dim and chilly cement-floored room crowded with huge stainless-steel tanks, a dense forest of massive silver tree trunks. The metal is cool to the touch, its dimpled surface dotted with beads of sweat. Lanky, bearded Eric strides through the gloom, beaker in hand, and pours two wine glasses three-quarters full of purple-red liquid. He and his guest swirl the wine to aerate it, opening up its aroma, then put their noses into their glasses. Inhaling deeply, the guest detects a rich, familiar scent. "Ahh, black cherry," she says, and Eric smiles.

117

They slurp, drawing the wine across their tongues with enough air to overcome any lingering shyness. Eric's guest tilts back her head and lets the wine touch every part of her mouth for several delicious seconds; then she leans over and aims a dark stream at the floor. This wine is still in the tank, but its beautifully rounded complexity is already in evidence. The guest smiles. "This is going to be wonderful," she says. But of course the winemaker already knows that. The inky elixir they've just tasted is slowly evolving into the Lenz Winery's 2004 Estate Merlot. The grapes that went into it came from vines fifteen to sixteen years old—teenagers, according to Eric.

"Vines age like humans," he says. "From three to ten they're like exuberant, playful children, and the wines made from them are full of bright and lively fruit flavors. Then they enter adolescence, and they get a bit more serious. The wines start to show more complexity and nuance." When they enter adulthood, around age twenty, the vines produce grapes that, in the right hands, create fabulous wines. "Like adult humans," says Eric, "they're more focused, more restrained, more interesting, intense, and elegant."

Old vines, he adds, produce smaller crops of the best grapes. Fruit from the most mature vines at Lenz goes into its Old Vines series, like the incipient 2005 Old Vines Chardonnay Eric and his visitor tasted from the tank before starting on the reds. "That's made from the best clones, the best blocks, and the ripest grapes," he says.

Lenz has a unique way of demonstrating the quality of its wines: independently controlled blind tastings of the best Lenz reds against the best of France. At the New York Yacht Club in Manhattan on March 15, 2006, Lenz's Merlot bested Château Figeac; its Cabernet Sauvignon edged out Château Latour; and its Old Vines Merlot came in very close behind Château Pétrus, whose most expensive bottle runs $2,650. Lenz has done the same with its white and sparkling wines, with similarly impressive results.

In most years the winery produces three Chardonnays: White Label, Gold Label, and Old Vines. Whites and sparkling wines produced in most years include Blanc de Noir, Gewürztraminer, and Méthode Champenoise Cuvée.

In reds Lenz currently produces Merlot and Cabernet Sauvignon; Estate Selection and Old Vines bottlings are produced from the best vintages.

The Lenz Winery
Main Road, Peconic
(631) 734-6010
office@lenzwine.com
www.lenzwine.com
Open year-round
Owners: Peter and Deborah Carroll
Winemaker: Eric Fry
Founded: 1978
Varieties grown: Chardonnay, Gewürztraminer, Cabernet Franc, Cabernet Sauvignon, Malbec, Merlot, Pinot Noir
Long Island Wine Council member

RAPHAEL

RISING OUT OF ITS NEATLY TRIMMED VINEYARD, RAPHAEL'S SPRAWLING ITALIANATE WINERY MAKES AN INDELIBLE IMPRESSION. OWNED BY Jack and Joan Petrocelli and named for Jack's father, Raphael was designed to resemble the monasteries near Naples, Italy, where the Petrocelli family has its roots.

The monastery theme is carried over to the entrance sign on the Main Road, flanked in midsummer by a profusion of orange daylilies. A fountain complete with cupids adorns the parking area. Entering the tasting room through large, arched double doors beneath a portico, you step into a vast hall, where open beams and a high ceiling draw the eye upward to tiered metalwork chandeliers and a double set of mezzanines.

Straight ahead, across a floor of muted tile, stands a circular tasting bar of blond wood. With its vertical pattern and three bands of gleaming silver metal, the bar is reminiscent of a traditional wooden wine vat. Beyond it a wall of doors and windows gives onto a vista of vines stretching toward the bay. Beneath your feet lies a cavernous, vaulted barrel cellar.

The Winemaker, Richard Olsen-Harbich

Rich Olsen-Harbich, who has been making wine on Long Island since 1982, is well known in the region not only for his skill and longevity, but also for preparing the complex petitions required to obtain Long Island's three official AVAs, or American Viticultural Areas: Long Island; North Fork of

Long Island; and the Hamptons, Long Island.

On a cold and drizzly February morning, a guest joins Rich in his tidy, subterranean lab to talk about his personal and professional journey as a local winemaker.

A native of Long Island, Rich grew up in New Hyde Park, near the border of Nassau and Suffolk Counties. His parents were of German heritage. "I was raised Old World," he says. "My grandparents lived with us, and there was always a lot of emphasis around food and gardening and flowers and the outdoors."

Like many area winemakers, Rich's first interest in growing things was more general than specific. At Cornell University, in New York's Finger Lakes wine region, he earned a degree in agronomy, the study of soil management and field crops.

"Then I changed over; my junior year I went into more viticulture," Rich says. "In the Finger Lakes I got exposed to the wine industry and really got interested in it—the ties to the Old World and the creative aspect of it. I was always a creative person, and the science aspect of it I was always interested in. It kind of tied all those interests together. Food and romance are also in there. I felt that I was returning to my roots."

In the Finger Lakes Rich worked with famed winemaker Hermann Wiemer. "I apprenticed with him for two years," he says. "And while I was working on the Island, I went up and did some training with him.

"I started working in the industry in 1981, working with the Mudds in the field and doing vineyard installations," Rich says. "At that time they were putting in hundreds and hundreds of acres of vines for different people. . . . I sat on the back of a planter and really got into it from the ground up, with posts and trellises." The Mudds Rich speaks of are vineyard experts well known on the East End.

Rich has been working in the Long Island wine industry his entire career, more than twenty-seven years. He first made wine on his own at Bridgehampton Winery, which went under in the early years of the region. "Bridgehampton was actually the second winery that opened on Long Island," Rich tells his guest. "We were selling wines from the 1982 vintage. Lyle Greenfield, who was the owner of that operation, was a crazy New York ad guy, and he gave me the opportunity to say, 'Hey, this is your product; create it and go with it.'

"So at that time I was managing the vineyard and making the wine," Rich continues. "I was twenty-two, and I had a lot of energy. People would ask me, because I was in the Hamptons all the time, 'That's great! You must be going out all time!' And I was like, 'Are you kidding? I don't know anything about it! I'm putting in eighty hours a week!' "

After Bridgehampton Winery was sold, Rich had to decide what to do next. "We had an opportunity to go different places, but my wife and I love Long Island," he says. An opportunity arose at Hargrave Vineyard, so Rich and his family moved to the North Fork, where he worked at a number of wineries and started a consulting business—which is how he met the Petrocellis, who wanted to establish a top-of-the-line vineyard and winery.

"Mr. Petrocelli and I discussed what he wanted to do, and it was a fantastic plan," Rich says. Drawing on his long experience in the region, Rich helped bring Raphael to fruition, so to speak.

"Steve Mudd and I were actually the principal people involved in getting this project under way. Steve helped pick the property with Jack Petrocelli, and then they brought me on board to consult on the wine operations."

The vineyard was planted in 1996, and Raphael opened its doors in 2001.

"I saw the potential for making a real statement with this company, with this facility, with the goals of the vineyard," Rich says. "We made a conscious effort to focus on varieties that we felt were successful. By the mid-1990s we knew that the way to go was not to make eighteen or twenty different kinds of wine. That was one idea, one plan that might have been stronger on a retail level, but on a quality level, I felt strongly that the region needed to put the best varieties first and work up from there, because any great wine region does that. They go with their strongest varieties, not what people want to make or like to drink. That's not necessarily what is going to be the best choice for a vineyard. You have to let the vineyard decide, let the soil and climate decide.

"By that time we really had a pretty good understanding," Rich goes on, "and Merlot was an obvious one. There was always a lot of tinkering that had to be done with the other varieties. They didn't come in quite ripe enough, or in balance. Merlot just looked like—at the top of the class, sailing through, like the kid who doesn't need much assistance in school. So it was a natural, and that was the case most years, even with our vintage variations.

"The North Fork has always, to me, had the potential to produce some of the best reds in the country," Rich declares, "and clearly, right now, we're the only region in the Northeast that can produce any kind of powerful, substantial red wines at all. I think that's a powerful advantage, and it would be foolish not to take advantage of it."

we make a special product, but it doesn't have to be looked upon in a special way to be appreciated.

"The interesting part is, when I deal with people at the retail store," he continues, "more than half the people will immediately say, 'I don't know anything about wine; I'm not a wine connoisseur.' And I say, 'I'm not a wine connoisseur, either; I'm a winemaker.' So they'll go through it, and I'll pour a bunch of different wines and they'll typically like the ones that I think are the best wines, the most expensive.

"I think most people can follow what it's all about," he says. "What has hampered us is the inability to get through all the noise and static that surround us every day and pay attention to things like this, pay attention to taste. It's not the American way to pay attention to taste and good food, necessarily. It's coming around, though; it's much better than it was."

"People have to trust themselves," says Rich. "They just need to relax, and if they want to have a white, a Sauvignon Blanc, with a steak, there's nothing wrong with that. There are so many rules; I think it's hampered America's appreciation for wine."

Rich feels that harvesting grapes by hand is vital to the quality of the wine. "Hand-harvesting gives us the ability to make decisions when one section is ripe and another one isn't," he says.

When the conversation turns to the tasting room, Rich says, "For the most part, people coming out want to find out more about wine. I've always tried to approach it as, this is not something you need to have a special education for; this is your taste buds and your ability to know what you like. I think

The Wines

About his winemaking philosophy Rich says, "I'm more or less hands-off in the wine cellar, but I'm completely hands on in the vineyard. That's where the wine is really being produced."

"The wines that I produce here, they are what they are," he says a moment later. "I don't add acid, take away acid, change any chemistry. I've been there, done that, and I don't think it's a sincere approach. I believe in the region producing the wine that it can produce, and I think that's a truer expression of what it is, like it or not."

Paul Pontellier, managing director of the famed Château Margaux in France's Bordeaux region, has been Raphael's winemaking consultant from the beginning, working with Rich to achieve the quality and style of wine they want.

"What I look for with red wines," Rich says, "number one is a very high level of ripeness: ripe, rich fruit flavors. It's a hedonistic level of taste that I'm looking for—a roundness, a softness, almost a fatness, an oiliness. Paul Pontellier calls it 'baby fat.' And it should be pleasant in a very sensuous way: a lot of flavor, not a sharp, tannic feel to it.

"For the most part, with our white wines, they're going to be very crisp and aromatic, very refreshing and thirst-quenching and bright. That's what I'm shooting for. I don't use oak on most of my white wines. I think it takes away from it.

"Cabernet Franc," he says, returning to the reds, "is one that I've gone in the direction of not using oak at all. My approach with that is that the fruity character, the softness of the wine, to me, is hidden with the use of oak barrels.

"With Merlot," Rich continues, "which is a much more powerful wine, it really benefits from oak aging. With that we're looking for very dark, complex flavors. Sometimes they're earthy, eucalyptus-like, sometimes chocolate and minty, but ultimately they should be mouth filling; it should give an impression of a velvety feel, but with some tannin to give it structure. We want it to be able to stand up to food. Some of them are not necessarily as easy to drink all by themselves, but that's really not what they're for.

When you have duck or a steak, that's really what they're made for."

Raphael's wines have received superlative reviews from the beginning, with especially high praise going to its signature Merlot and, more recently, its Cabernet Franc. Reds offered in most years include First Label Merlot; La Fontana, a blend of Merlot, Petit Verdot, and Cabernet Franc; Bel Rosso, a mostly Cabernet Franc blend; Estate Merlot; and Cabernet Franc. A new release is Vino Pestato, made from Petit Verdot with a little Merlot and pressed the old-fashioned way, by treading underfoot. Merliance, a premium Bordeaux blend created by the Long Island Merlot Alliance, of which Raphael is a member, is also available.

A dry rosé, Saignée, is made from Merlot. Two whites are available at this writing: Sauvignon Blanc and Grand Cru, a stainless-steel-fermented 100 percent Chardonnay.

Raphael
Main Road, Peconic
(631) 765-1100
info@raphaelwine.com
www.raphaelwine.com
Open year-round; Saturdays by appointment only
Owners: Jack and Joan Petrocelli
Winemaker: Richard Olsen-Harbich
Founded: 1996
Acres planted: 60
Varieties grown: Sauvignon Blanc, Cabernet Franc, Cabernet Sauvignon, Malbec, Merlot, Petit Verdot
Long Island Wine Council member

ACKERLY POND VINEYARDS

UITE A FEW LONG ISLAND TASTING ROOMS ARE CONVERTED FARM BUILDINGS; THE CENTURY-OLD BARN AT ACKERLY POND VINEYARDS ON Peconic Lane is as authentic as they come. The silver-gray structure with its high-peaked roof proclaiming PECONIC, L.I., N.Y. is a North Fork landmark.

The tasting room is entered through the original sliding barn door. One of the smallest tasting rooms on the East End, it makes up in unstudied rustic charm what it lacks in size. Except for sweeping out the dust and cobwebs and putting in a counter, the owners left the barn in its natural state, complete with weathered walls, decades-old calendars, cattle inspection signs, and assorted farming tools. An old wooden winepress stands near the end of the counter.

Ackerly Pond Vineyards is named after a pond about a mile to the east, where a gristmill once ground grain into flour. The ambience here is down-home, small-town friendly. Most often you'll find owner Jill Blum's stepdaughter, Kerri Blum, behind the bar.

The Owner, Jill Blum

The late Ray Blum was one of the East End wine region's most beloved and enthusiastic pioneers.

Although he made his living in the airline industry, a passion for green and growing things was in his blood.

On a cold, wet, windy morning in January, Jill Blum, a lovely woman with a slight build, fair hair, and porcelain complexion, sits down with a visitor in the spacious kitchen of the renovated farmhouse just steps from the barn tasting room. After her four papillons—Teddy, Waffles, Dallas, and Desi—get over the excitement of having a guest in the house, Jill talks about Ray, how he came to be a grower of grapes on eastern Long Island, and how his vineyard life became hers, too.

"You might say he was looking for an adventure," she begins. "He did have a background in horticulture. He had a landscaping company with his brother in the Sayville-Oakdale area when they were teenagers. When they both got drafted, they sold the business. After they came back from Vietnam, they planned to continue their parents' business, a Dairy Queen in Hicksville, but they found out their parents had sold the Dairy Queen, moved out to Mattituck, and bought the Mattituck Motel, which they ran for many, many years back in—oh, I'd say the 1960s and '70s. They finally sold it and moved to Florida."

While visiting his parents in Mattituck, Ray discovered the North Fork. "He would come out and spend a lot of time here, and he grew to love the area, like a lot of people do," Jill says. "Then, when he was looking for his adventure, I guess he kind of went back to his original talent, which was horticulture. I think a friend of his read something in the newspaper, after the Hargraves opened, that mentioned vineyards. That sparked Ray's interest and he came out here, looked at a lot of properties— most of the properties are the other vineyards that

are built now—and he settled on one across from the shopping center in Cutchogue, which is of course Peconic Bay. He planted that in 1979."

Jill met Ray in 1985. She was a microbiologist and he was an air traffic controller, a career path he had followed since his stint in the armed forces. According to Jill, he had no illusions about making a living from his vineyard.

"Ray had always wanted to do something else," Jill says. "There was his job, and then he wanted something to be his hobby, I guess."

The two married in 1998. In 1999 Ray sold Peconic Bay Winery and started Ackerly Pond Vineyards, planting sixteen acres in Peconic and sixty-five acres in Southold. Not long after that, Jill

quit her job to help Ray manage the vineyards and tasting room.

"This was sod when we bought it," she says of the land. "We planted it right away, even before we moved in, to get the vines established and growing. Ray and I worked at it, and we really had a lot of fun running this farm. We really did." She laughs and adds, "Ray always liked these huge quantities of grapes. I was always saying, 'Don't plant so much!' But he liked it like that. He liked big fields and tons and tons of grapes. We would take the dogs and walk up and down the rows together."

After Ray died in January 2007, Jill hired a vineyard manager. She plans to sell the larger Southold vineyard but has decided to keep the Peconic property she fondly calls "the farm." She wasn't so fond of it when they first bought the place, though.

"The barn was in pretty good shape," Jill recalls, "but the property itself was not in good shape. The house was very run down, really badly run down. We actually didn't want the house, but it came as one big package, so we really couldn't cut it out. Basically it was standing, and that was about it." A lot of time and renovation went into making the old farmhouse the snug and handsome dwelling it is today.

When her visitor asks what kept her and Ray going through the hard times, Jill smiles and shakes her head. "This may sound silly," she says, "but I don't remember many hard times. Some years were better than others. I think he would have been very pleased about the 2007 harvest, which was spectacular. I guess the biggest disappointment was 2005, when we got the rains. That was really incredible."

Jill is referring to the colossal storm that drenched the East End with nine straight days of rain in October 2005. A lot of the red crop was lost, but much of what was left on the vine over the dry, breezy days that followed ultimately produced intensely flavored wines of rare complexity.

With the vineyard in capable hands, Jill has time to pursue two of her passions: painting and showing her dogs in agility trials. "Dallas and Desi show; Teddy and Waffles are retired," Jill says. "Ray came to some of my dog shows, but without Ray I keep myself a little bit busier. I got another puppy, Desi, and his training keeps me busy."

Last summer Jill showed her dogs all over the Northeast, traveling in her van with a schoolteacher friend. "She has the third-best agility dog in the nation," Jill says. "We traveled all around. We went to

Ohio twice, Albany, Syracuse, Burlington, Vermont, New Jersey, Pennsylvania—we went everywhere, all summer. We had a good time; we're going to do it again this year."

Jill's other passion, painting, has become a second business: painting portraits of beloved pets. Her talent with oils is evident in the examples on her walls and the awards she's won.

The Wines

Ray was growing Cabernet Sauvignon, Merlot, and Riesling when Jill joined him at his first vineyard. "I still have some of those bottles downstairs," she says. "I thought they were pretty good, even back in the 1980s. And now we have all these talented winemakers out here."

One of those talented winemakers is Eric Fry of the Lenz Winery; he crafts Ackerly Pond's award-winning, food-friendly wines. Currently in the tasting room are two vintages of Merlot, a Cabernet Franc, and a Chardonnay.

The 2003 Merlot, a gold-medal winner at the 2005 New York Wine and Food Classic, was aged for fourteen months in small French oak barrels and shows true varietal characteristics of blackberry and currants. The 2004 Merlot is elegant and medium-bodied, with aromatic hints of smoky oak and characteristic flavors of blackberry and chocolate. The ripely fruity and aromatic 2003 Cabernet Franc, which took silver at the 2005 New York Wine and Food Classic, tastes of raspberries and spice. The fresh and fruity oaked 2006 Chardonnay is medium-bodied, with flavors of green apple, pear, and vanilla.

Ackerly Pond Vineyards
1375 Peconic Lane, Peconic
(631) 765-6861
rayvin5@aol.com
www.ackerlypondvineyards.com
Open year-round
Owner: Jill Blum
Winemaker: Eric Fry
Founded: 1999
Acres planted: 81
Varieties grown: Chardonnay, Cabernet Franc, Cabernet Sauvignon, Merlot
Long Island Wine Council member

Spring Onion, Potato, and Goat Cheese Tart

The North Fork Table & Inn, Southold | *Claudia Fleming, pastry chef*

Tart Dough

- 1¼ cups all-purpose flour
- ½ teaspoon salt
- 2 tablespoons very cold vegetable shortening
- 6 tablespoons (3 ounces) cold, unsalted butter, cut into ½-inch cubes
- ¼ cup ice water

Tart Filling

- 2 tablespoons butter
- 1 pound red spring onions, cut in half and sliced ⅛-inch thick
- 8 ounces fingerling potatoes, sliced into ¼-inch discs
- 1 clove garlic
- 1 sprig rosemary
- Salt and pepper
- 1 tablespoon fresh thyme leaves, plus sprigs for garnish
- 1 ounce extra-virgin olive oil (preferably Umbrian), plus more for drizzling on tart
- 4 ounces goat cheese*

*Chef Fleming recommends cheese from Catapano Dairy Farm in Peconic.

1. In the bowl of a food processor, combine flour, salt, shortening, and butter. Pulse until mixture resembles coarse meal and the butter pieces are the size of peas. Turn out into a large bowl and drizzle the water in. Toss mixture with a fork until it looks lumpy and gnarly.
2. Turn mixture out onto a lightly floured board and gently gather into a single mass of dough. Transfer onto a large sheet of plastic wrap, enclose in plastic, and press into a disc with a rolling pin. Refrigerate for at least 1 hour.
3. Preheat oven to 350°F. On a lightly floured work surface, roll out tart dough into a 14 x 13-inch rectangle ⅛ inch thick. Fit into square tart pan, leaving a ½-inch overhang. Fold overhang under and press against rim of pan to form a reinforced edge.
4. Prick bottom of tart shell lightly all over with a fork, line with foil or parchment, and fill shell with dried beans or uncooked rice. Bake for 20 minutes, then remove liner and beans/rice and bake about 10 minutes longer to allow even browning.
5. In a heavy-bottomed sauté pan over medium-high heat, melt butter. Add onions and cook, stirring occasionally, until onions are caramelized. Set aside.
6. Place potatoes in a pot and cover with cold water; add garlic, rosemary, and salt and pepper to taste. Bring to a boil and cook until just tender. Drain and let cool to room temperature.
7. Place potatoes and onions in a stainless-steel bowl and toss together with the thyme leaves and olive oil.
8. Place filling in the blind-baked shell, top with goat cheese, and bake at 350°F until goat cheese is soft and beginning to brown, approximately 20 minutes.
9. Garnish with fresh thyme sprigs and drizzle with olive oil.

Serves 9–12. Serve warm or at room temperature. Pair with a Long Island Riesling or Sauvignon Blanc.

THE TASTING ROOM

PECONIC'S HAMLET CENTER IS ONE OF THE TINIEST ON THE NORTH FORK, WITH A SINGLE ROW OF SMALL SHOPS AND A POST OFFICE ON the west side of Peconic Lane. One of those quaint shops, built in the 1860s, has been turned into the East End's only multiwinery tasting room. Operated by Theresa Dilworth, owner of Comtesse Thérèse, the Tasting Room showcases wines from several of the North Fork's smaller producers, including Comtesse Thérèse, Bouké, Bridge Vineyards, Christiano Family Vineyards, Medolla Vineyards, Schneider Vineyards, and Sparkling Pointe.

You'll find more information on Comtesse Thérèse in the Aquebogue section of this book. Three additional winemakers not listed here are featured under Small Producers of the North Fork.

The Tasting Room
Peconic Lane, Peconic
(631) 765-6404
mail@tastingroomli.com
www.tastingroomli.com
Open year-round

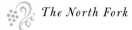

BOUKÉ

Long Island native Lisa Donneson, a wine enthusiast who has been granted Diploma status by the prestigious Wine and Spirits Education Trust, has teamed up with award-winning, French-born winemaker Gilles Martin to produce a new line of wines under the name Bouké, a playful twist on the wine term *bouquet*.

Lisa says her goal is to create complex, aromatic, well-balanced wines for everyday drinking pleasure, wines that express Long Island's unique influence. Gilles has convinced her that blends are the best way to achieve that aim.

As of this writing, two wines have been released under the distinctive, color-striped Bouké label. Crisp, stainless-steel-fermented 2007 Bouké White blends Chardonnay, Pinot Gris, Sauvignon Blanc, and Gewürztraminer. The 2007 Bouké Rosé, also fermented in steel, is a fruity, aromatic marriage of Cabernet Sauvignon and Merlot. Slated for release in January 2009, full-bodied 2007 Bouké Red is a blend of Cabernet Franc, Merlot, Cabernet Sauvignon, Syrah, and Petit Verdot.

Bouké wines are produced at Premium Wine Group in Mattituck with fruit purchased from North Fork vineyards.

Bouké

(877) 877-0527
lisa@boukewines.com
www.boukewines.com
Owner: Lisa Donneson
Winemaker: Gilles Martin
Long Island Wine Council member

BRIDGE VINEYARDS

Bridge Vineyards is unique among Long Island wineries: Although its vineyard is in Cutchogue and most of its wine is produced at Premium Wine Group in Mattituck, its main tasting room and urban winery are in Brooklyn, in the shadow of the Williamsburg Bridge. Bridge Urban Winery offers wine and food pairings featuring its own wines and others from New York State, and it hosts dinners and educational events.

Co-owners Greg Sandor and Paul Wegimont pay meticulous attention in the vineyard, hand-harvesting the grapes, and then handcraft Bridge wines in small lots. Their winemaker is Eric Fry of the Lenz Winery.

Bridge Vineyards' award-winning estate wines include 2001 Merlot, 2003 Merlot, 2002 Cabernet Sauvignon, and 2005 Chardonnay. Reserve Merlot and Riesling are also currently on the wine list, along with easy-drinking, nonvintage table wines under the Brooklyn Bridge label: Brooklyn Red and Brooklyn White.

Bridge Vineyards

(718) 384-2800
greg@bridgevineyards.com
paul@bridgevineyards.com
www.bridgevineyards.com
Owners: Greg Sandor and Paul Wegimont
Winemaker: Eric Fry
Long Island Wine Council member

Brooklyn tasting room:

Bridge Urban Winery
20 Broadway Avenue
Williamsburg, Brooklyn
Open year-round

CHRISTIANO FAMILY VINEYARDS

Claude Christiano started out as a collector of fine wines, then helped to found Monte de Oro Vineyards in Southern California before realizing his dream of planting a vineyard and making wine on the North Fork of Long Island.

A former vice president and assistant treasurer of Pfizer Inc., Claude has visited wine regions around the world, sampling wines and learning about grape-growing and winemaking. After he retired several years ago, he purchased seven acres of Southold farmland and planted top-quality Merlot, Cabernet Sauvignon, and Chardonnay vines.

Christiano Family Vineyards' first and second releases, 2004 Merlot and 2006 Chardonnay, both well received by wine writers, are available in the Tasting Room as this is written. Premium Wine Group in Mattituck produced these wines.

Christiano Family Vineyards
info@christianowines.com
www.christianowines.com
Owner: Claude Christiano
Winemaker: Premium Wine Group
Long Island Wine Council member

MEDOLLA VINEYARDS

John and Denise Medolla, both airline industry professionals, are continuing a long family tradition of winemaking that goes back to John's ancestors, who lived in the shadow of Italy's Mount Vesuvius.

The Medollas purchase fruit from North Fork growers, including Sam McCullough, vineyard manager at the Lenz Winery in Peconic, who has his own vineyard in Aquebogue. They then work closely with Lenz winemaker Eric Fry to handcraft

wines that express their family's Old World heritage, focusing on their passion, Merlot.

Medolla Vineyards' first release, the 2002 Merlot, won a silver medal at the 2007 New York Wine and Food Classic, won a bronze medal at the 2007 Atlantic Seaboard Wine Competition, garnered 88 points in the influential *Wine Spectator,* and received good reviews in other wine publications. Medolla Vineyards makes five hundred cases a year.

Medolla Vineyards
(631) 334-3059
info@medollavineyards.com
www.medollavineyards.com
Owners: John and Denise Medolla
Winemaker: Eric Fry

SCHNEIDER VINEYARDS

Schneider Vineyards is unique on Long Island for its singular focus on producing world-class Cabernet Franc, which owners Bruce and Christiane Baker Schneider believe to be the varietal best suited to the region. They began making wine on the North Fork in 1994, using purchased grapes. Subsequently, they planted a vineyard in Riverhead that they sold several years later.

Starting with the 2007 vintage, the fruit for Schneider Vineyards' very limited-production estate wines is from the eleven-acre Jackson Hill Vineyard in Mattituck, planted in 2002. Most of the wines are produced at Premium Wine Group in Mattituck. Bruce comes from a family of wine importers, but he is the first of three generations in the wine business to make wine.

Schneider Vineyards' wine is served in leading Long Island and New York City restaurants, including the American Hotel in Sag Harbor and Chanterelle and Le Bernardin in Manhattan, and can be found at some Manhattan wine shops.

These wines have received outstanding reviews from critics since the first vintage in 1994. The latest releases as of this writing, all from the 2005 vintage, are Cabernet Franc Le Breton, Cabernet Franc Le Bouchet, Cabernet Franc–Petit Verdot, and Cabernet Franc La Cloche.

Schneider Vineyards
www.tastingroomli.com/schneider.htm
Owners: Bruce and Christiane Baker Schneider
Winemakers: Bruce Schneider and Premium Wine Group

SPARKLING POINTE

At Sparkling Pointe the traditional *méthode champenoise* is followed to produce Champagne-style sparkling wines. That, in itself, is not unusual on Long Island. What is unusual, even unique, is that sparkling wine is all they produce.

Owners Tom and Cynthia Rosicki, both attorneys, say the idea for Sparkling Pointe was born from their love of the country life, romance, and Champagne. Residents of the North Fork, they watched the beginnings and growth of the nascent wine region and decided they wanted to become part of it.

In 2002 they purchased twelve acres on Route 48 in Southold and planted the classic Champagne grapes: Chardonnay, Pinot Noir, and Pinot Meunier. Gilles Martin, a French-born winemaker who worked for a famous French Champagne house, was hired as their consultant.

While waiting for their vines to mature, they purchased top-quality fruit and produced their first two releases: 2004 Sparkling Pointe Brut and 2004 Sparkling Pointe Topaz Imperial. Both have been well received by wine critics; Topaz Imperial was named Best Sparkling Wine at the 2008 Wine Literary Awards. These wines were made by Gilles Martin at Premium Wine Group in Mattituck.

A 2009 opening is projected for Sparkling Pointe's production facility and a wine-tasting center designed by Cutchogue architect Nancy Steelman.

Sparkling Pointe
(631) 316-0530
gmartin@sparklingpointe.com
www.sparklingpointe.com
Owners: Tom and Cynthia Rosicki
Winemaker: Gilles Martin
Long Island Wine Council member

OSPREY'S DOMINION

OSPREYS ARE A FAMILIAR SIGHT ON THE EAST END. LOCALS WATCH FOR THEIR RETURN IN EARLY SPRING, WHEN THEY RECLAIM THEIR lofty nests, fashioned on a base of branches affixed by human hands to a platform at the top of a pole. In the wild they nest in trees, but eastern Long Island is no longer a wild place. All through the spring and summer these fish hawks soar high above our bays and creeks, seeking the silver flash of a fish in the water far below. An osprey's plummeting, talon-first dive is thrilling to watch. A splash, a pumping of

powerful wings, and the bird is aloft again, carrying its catch to the nest to feed its hungry young.

The winery that bears its name is heralded by a lifelike sculpture of an osprey in the moment of landing on its nest. Twin ospreys are etched on the glass doors of the main entrance to the tasting room. And of course Osprey's Dominion wines bear the hawk's image on their labels.

That wasn't how it began, though. Before owners Bud Koehler and Bill Tyree officially started their new business, they were planning to call it Richmond

Creek, after a saltwater creek near the property. But in 1983, the official year of its founding, "Osprey's Dominion" seemed a more compelling, and certainly more romantic, choice.

The simple entrance to the tasting room belies what you'll find inside. There the view opens up to an expansive space with a generous, curving tasting bar of blond wood and a wall of windows beneath a soaring, heavy-beamed cathedral ceiling. Windowed side walls and skylights flood this indoor patio with abundant light, inviting guests to linger over a glass of wine at one of the many tables. Outdoors it's just as inviting, with an open-air patio, acres of grass, picnic tables, and a charmingly rustic vine-draped gazebo.

The Owners, Bud Koehler and Bill Tyree

Bud Koehler and Bill Tyree, both Long Island natives, have been best friends ever since they met at Holy Name of Mary school in Valley Stream. "I've known Bill since he was seven years old," says Bud.

Bill picks up the story. "He'd come over to my house, throw some pebbles at the house early in the morning, and we'd be gone all day."

"I'd walk a mile to his house and we'd go hunting rabbits or something," Bud adds.

By their own accounts, they were quite the pair. "We got into a lot of trouble," Bill declares with a chuckle, "but we never got arrested. Today if you did what we used to do, you'd be in jail! But they were just pranks. Nobody got hurt."

Their tandem lives continued into adulthood, in business and in leisure. Each owned a successful construction business before retiring. They did construction projects together and bought real estate together. And they share a consuming passion for small planes. Both Bud and Bill are pilots who have owned several vintage airplanes, including a rebuilt 1942 Stearman biplane and a Russian Sukhoi monoplane. They even did air shows together. Once they get going on their aeronautical adventures, you'd better settle in for a while, but it's a real treat to listen to their stories and easy banter.

They also share a passion for their families.

"I have eleven children . . ." says Bud.

Bill chimes in before his friend can finish his sentence: "I have eight."

". . . and twenty-nine grandchildren," Bud continues smoothly, as if the interruption had never happened. "And we have four great-grandchildren. It's a good crew. When the Koehler group gets together on my lawn in New Suffolk—just the Koehlers—there's fifty people there."

"I have four granddaughters getting married this year," Bill says.

Bud shakes his head in wonder. "It's amazing, isn't it? You turn around and you say, 'Which one is that?'"

When a guest asks the two old friends what made them decide to plant a vineyard on the North Fork, Bud answers for them both. "I'd been out here, and we always boated and loved the Island. I could never move away from here. If I didn't think I could put one foot out and get it in the water . . ."

He breaks off, then continues, his voice a mixture of enthusiasm and consternation. "I think half the people who live on the Island don't know where they live. I really mean it—this place is so beautiful. The waterways you have around here are so gorgeous, so beautiful, that it's hard to find something to really replace it."

After a pause Bud talks about planting his first vineyard at the urging of his friend and attorney Jack Gillies. Jack's son, Matt, who started working for the Hargraves as a teenager, became Osprey's first vineyard manager. For a few years Bud and Bill sold all the grapes they grew.

"I kept developing it," says Bud, "and then I bought the piece of land on Locust Avenue and planted some grapes up in there. So we took some grapes and we weren't going to sell them, so I said, well, let's make some wine out of them!"

That was around 1988, Bud recalls. At first they made the wine on the South Fork, at the winery that later became Duck Walk. "We were thinking about purchasing that place, but we came over here and this property was for sale. They had a barn, but they didn't make wine here, and they had some vineyards in the back, so Bill and I bought it."

After they set up their new winery in the barn, the first vintage was produced in 1991.

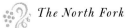

The Winemaker, Adam Suprenant, and Vineyard Manager, Tom Stevenson

Adam Suprenant and Tom Stevenson are both graduates of the University of California, Davis, home of a renowned enology program. Adam holds a master's in winemaking; Tom's degree is in agricultural systems with an emphasis on viticulture. Eventually chance and opportunity landed both men at Osprey's Dominion, where their teamwork led to the winery's being crowned Winery of the Year at the 2005 New York Wine and Food Classic.

Adam's winemaking philosophy revolves around finding the right balance between such opposing elements as tannins, alcohol, and acidity. Like other winemakers, he acknowledges the necessity of bringing in good fruit from the vineyard. "There's no way to make great wine from poor-quality grapes," he says. "The vineyard gives you the base."

That's where Tom comes in. As long as the grapes are on the vine, he says, they're his responsibility. From winter pruning to summer spraying to fall harvest, Tom oversees all of Osprey's Dominion's vineyards, working closely with Adam to judge optimum ripeness for each variety and decide when to pick.

After harvest Adam takes over, aiming for wines that express the character they developed in the vineyard rather than the heavy hand of the winemaker. He dismisses any notion of glamour or romance in winemaking. "The glory of winemaking has been overdone by wine writers," he declares. "You're at the mercy of yeast and bacteria."

The Wines

Osprey's Dominion produces about twelve thousand cases a year. Its long wine list runs the gamut from light and fruity crowd-pleasers to medal-winning varietals and premium blends. Varietals include Sauvignon Blanc, oaked and unoaked Chardonnay, Gewürztraminer, Riesling, Pinot Noir, Merlot, Cabernet Franc, Cabernet Sauvignon, Port, Rosé, sweet table wine, and peach, strawberry, and spice wines. Reserve versions of Chardonnay and Merlot are produced from the best vintages.

Richmond Creek Red, an easy-drinking, dry table wine, is a top seller and a favorite of the owners. "You go into any Italian restaurant and pour that in a pitcher," says Bill, "they'll swear the owner made that. That's the best Italian homemade wine they've ever had in their life!"

Osprey's Dominion
Main Road, Peconic
(631) 765-6188 or (888) 295-6188
odvtastingroom@optonline.net
www.ospreysdominion.com
Open year-round
Owners: Bud Koehler and Bill Tyree
Winemaker: Adam Suprenant
Founded: 1983
Acres planted: 90
Varieties grown: Chardonnay, Riesling, Sauvignon Blanc, Cabernet Franc, Cabernet Sauvignon, Merlot, Pinot Noir
Long Island Wine Council member

COREY CREEK VINEYARDS

COREY CREEK'S TASTING ROOM APPEARS RATHER SMALL FROM THE OUTSIDE, BUT AN OPEN-BEAMED CATHEDRAL CEILING, ALONG with glass doors and tall windows overlooking the deck and vineyard, lend the interior a feeling of spaciousness. The tasting bar is topped with gleaming polished copper, and the blond wood on the walls enhances the sense of openness.

The tasting room is elevated above the landscape, offering stunning views of the vineyard. In midsummer row after row of green vines, framed above by the slatted roof of the deck, below by bushes heavy with pink roses, stretch across the landscape, seeming to converge at a distant line of trees.

Visitors will find live music here on warm-weather weekends and frequent exhibitions by local painters and photographers.

Founded in 1993, Corey Creek Vineyards was purchased in 1999 by Michael Lynne, co-chairman and co-CEO of New Line Cinema and executive producer of the *Lord of the Rings* trilogy, who also owns Bedell Cellars. The first eighteen acres were planted with Chardonnay by the previous owners. Merlot, Cabernet Franc, Gewürztraminer, and Pinot Noir went in later, for a total of thirty acres.

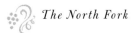

This wine was awarded a double gold medal and named Best Gewürztraminer at the 2005 New York Wine and Food Classic.

Corey Creek also produces Cabernet Franc and two of the North Fork's most popular and iconic table wines, Main Road Red and Main Road White. The labels on these fresh, lively, easy-drinking blends depict the venerable, bright-red pickup truck usually parked outside Bedell Cellars' tasting room.

Bright and crisp Domaines CC Rose is another customer favorite, and two dessert wines are currently offered: the exotic Late Harvest Riesling and the tangy Raspberry.

Corey Creek Vineyards
Main Road, Southold
(631) 765-4168
wine@coreycreek.com
www.coreycreek.com
Open year-round
Owner: Michael Lynne
Founding winemaker: Kip Bedell
Winemaker: Kelly Urbanik
Founded: 1993
Acres planted: 30
Varieties grown: Chardonnay, Cabernet Franc, Gewürztraminer, Merlot, Pinot Noir
Long Island Wine Council member

The Wines

Corey Creek's wines are produced at Bedell Cellars by founding winemaker Kip Bedell and winemaker Kelly Urbanik, in consultation with Pascal Marty. (See Bedell Cellars in the Cutchogue section.)

Corey Creek is especially known for its dry, aromatic, and complex Gewürztraminer, sourced from Bedell Cellars and Corey Creek's older vines.

DUCK WALK NORTH

THE TASTING ROOM AT DUCK WALK NORTH, ONE OF THE LARGEST ON THE EAST END, GIVES A NOD TO TRADITIONAL NORTH FORK architecture with its gabled roof lines and, inside, its open rafters, vaulted ceiling, and generous use of wood. Light floods in through arched windows in the southern wall, and a picture window in the north wall frames the vineyard. The surprise here is a large aquarium near the entrance, where colorful fish offer a glimpse of another world.

Like Duck Walk Vineyards, its counterpart in the Hamptons, Duck Walk North is owned by Dr. Herodotus "Dan" Damianos and family. The eldest son, Alexander, manages both businesses. One Saturday in May, Alex talked with a visitor about the origins of Duck Walk North.

"My family owned a piece of land about a mile down the road from Pindar, and we weren't doing anything with it," Alex says. "One of our intentions was to possibly build an extension of Duck Walk."

Then he tells an amusing story about getting his father to agree to the project while Dr. Dan was coming out of anesthesia after minor surgery. "I said, 'Dad, do you think I could get working on this project, Duck Walk North?' and he's like, 'Uh, okay.' The next day, I had the architect in the office. When my father got out of the hospital, I said, 'Dad, you know, you told me . . .' He said, 'I did? I don't remember that.' And I said, 'I already have the plans!' "

The tasting room, which opened in May 2007, was a success right out of the gate.

See Duck Walk Vineyards in the Hamptons section for information about Duck Walk's wines.

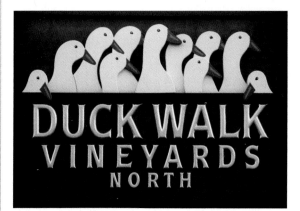

Duck Walk North
Main Road, Southold
(631) 765-3500
info@duckwalk.com
www.duckwalk.com
Open year-round
Long Island Wine Council member

THE OLD FIELD VINEYARDS

A MILE EAST OF SOUTHOLD'S HAMLET CENTER, A HANDSOME SIGN INSIDE A LOW, WHITE FENCE READS "THE OLD FIELD." TURNING DOWN A dirt drive, you come to a small parking area beneath lofty trees with branches almost as thick as their trunks. There's no tasting room in sight. Just when you're about to decide you've come to the wrong place, you spot the hand-painted sign, "TASTING ROOM." An arrow points across the grass.

As you approach the tiny tasting room, there's a low clucking sound behind you; you look around to see a rooster and a few chickens pecking the ground. In front of a large chicken coop, a duck feeds from a bowl. Out in the vineyard a man in a baseball cap drives an old riding mower between the rows. Later, you find out the guy on the mower owns the vineyard with his wife, who might be seen lugging cartons of wine bottles into the old dairy barn turned barrel

Chris Baiz carries grape lugs for the Chardonnay harvest.

cellar and bottling room. The lanky young woman wearing a red bandana, the one behind the tasting table on the shady deck, is their daughter. Welcome to the Old Field Vineyards.

This property on Southold Bay was farmed by Native Americans for at least five hundred years before the first European settlers arrived on these shores in 1640. The first records referencing the

Old Field date from the late seventeenth century.

Christian Baiz's great-great-grandmother bought the property as World War I came to a close, and it stayed in the family through the generations. After his grandmother died in 1993, the Old Field came into the hands of Chris and his wife, Rosamond Phelps Baiz. The elder generations planted their first vineyard in 1974 with Chardonnay cuttings purchased from Alex

Ros Baiz is right at home on the tractor.

and Louisa Hargrave. Pinot Noir was planted in 1985, followed by Merlot and Cabernet Franc in 1997, for a total of about twelve acres producing an average of a thousand cases of wine a year.

The Owners, Christian Baiz and Rosamond Phelps Baiz

As the fourth and fifth generations ·of the same family to own and work the Old Field, Chris and Ros Baiz and their daughter, Perry Weiss, take their responsibility as stewards of the land seriously. When he comes home for a visit, their son, Ryan, joins them in that responsibility. In fact, it was a shared determination to save the property from development that prompted them to buy it.

"We were living in Bronxville, in Westchester," Ros begins. "We were here one afternoon and overheard people talking about what they were going to do if they bought the property—development and

what it was going to consist of, this going up and the buildings all coming down. And it felt so extremely, extraordinarily bad to me. Chris and I had talked, and I knew this was his dream. I wasn't sure it was mine at the time, but that just killed me. I thought, 'No, no, no, no, no!' Perry had gone off to college, and we thought, why not?"

Chris adds, "There were so many different things, six or seven major events that all came within thirty days of each other, that just said we're being led in this direction."

But it was hard going at the outset. "I've had no farming background," Ros admits, "so it was pretty interesting at first. Chris would leave and go into Manhattan, and I'd sit there and look at the tractor and go, 'Uh-oh!' But we had this really nice neighbor across the street, and he'd come over. It was absolutely wonderful. The more I got into it, the more I loved it, and then Perry got sucked in.

Perry Weiss corks bottles the old-fashioned way, one at a time.

Now she loves it and wants to continue to do it."

Asked why she loves all the hard work, Ros says, "I think it's the land, being outside, watching it, trying to understand the soils, trying to understand how it all works together, to understand the harmony of nature. And it's an amazing thing to be able to make a product that pleasures people and that can sit on somebody's table and be part of their meal, part of their community—it's wonderful. And I love my chickens, too, so it works well!" she concludes with a delighted laugh.

Expounding on the same subject, Chris says, "I think the biggest thing is simply conserving the place. My mother grew up here, and my grandmother before my mother was born, so my mother has known this place all of her life, and my grandmother

since infancy. This is heaven's footprint. The idea isn't to change it and to make it look all done up to the nines, with everything absolutely pristinely manicured like a picture book, because that's not the way life was."

"This is a remnant of the farms on the bay that back onto the Main Road," he says later. "One of the others is right next door to us, and the third one is the Terry farm, and that's it. Everything else has been developed, and it's all been subdivided."

"I feel the same way my mom feels about conserving the land," says Perry. "This piece of property has so many different microenvironments. It's amazing what's on the property. There's a pond, the bay, the wooded lots. And we have so much diversity in the animal life. I think that's really unique out here—such a nice piece of land with so many different things on it. It's wonderful. And I think just to preserve this land—I'd never like to see a whole bunch of condominiums here."

Perry was planning to be a marine biologist and study sharks. "I soon found out that my grades needed to be a lot better and there was no money in it."

This elicits a wry comment from her father: "There's no money in farming, either."

Perry laughs. "Well, it's a little different," she says. "When I was in college, I didn't really like working in the field, but now, as I get older—Mom is my idol for being out there. She can work forever."

Ros starts to demur, but Perry insists. "You are, Mom. She can work just forever and never stop. And as I get older, I find I can work harder and harder. I'm next in line to take the place over, so I'm getting more and more involved. Mom and I are making the wine now."

One of Ros's favorite tasks is cutting back the vines. "I love wintertime pruning," she declares. "I can take my time out there and just enjoy the peace of the shears. Running a vineyard is lots of work and lots of enjoyment and lots of—I don't know. It's a fascinating way to live."

The Wines

The Old Field Vineyards produces about a thousand cases of Bordeaux and Burgundy-style wines each year. The current list includes Merlot, barrel- and steel-fermented Chardonnays, Cabernet Franc, Blush de Noir, Blanc de Noir sparkling wine, and Rooster Tail, a Bordeaux-blend red table wine. With only a few wines produced from each vintage, the focus here is strictly on quality. Almost all Old Field wine is sold directly to customers at the tasting room.

This small, family-run winery scored big with its 2000 Blanc de Noir when influential *Wine Advocate* gave it a score of 90.

Ros and Perry make the wine in consultation with master winemaker Eric Fry of the Lenz Winery.

The Old Field Vineyards
Main Road, Southold
(631) 765-0004
livinifera@aol.com
www.theoldfield.com
Open February through December
Owners: Christian Baiz and Rosamond Phelps Baiz
Winemakers: Eric Fry, Rosamond Baiz, and Perry Weiss
Founded: 1974
Acres planted: 12
Varieties grown: Chardonnay, Cabernet Franc, Merlot, Pinot Noir
Long Island Wine Council member

Boneless Marinated Duck Legs with Roasted Plum Sauce

Chef John Ross

1 cup orange juice

¼ cup soy sauce

¼ cup honey, plus more for basting

12 duck legs*

12 fresh plums, halved and pitted

3 cups Long Island Merlot

1 tablespoon maple syrup

½ cup chopped shallots

2 tablespoons beach plum jam or
    currant jelly

½ cup chicken broth

Coarse salt and pepper

*Chef Ross recommends Crescent Duck Farm in Aquebogue.

1. Whisk together orange juice, soy sauce, and honey to make marinade. Trim excess fat from the duck legs; discard the fat. Place the duck legs and marinade in a ziplock bag and refrigerate for 2 hours or more.

2. Meanwhile, preheat oven to 400°F. Place the halved and pitted plums cut-side down on a sheet pan. Combine 1 cup of the Merlot with the maple syrup and pour over the plums. Roast the plums for 20 minutes and allow to cool. Remove the skins from the plums and scrape out the flesh, reserving any juice.

3. In a saucepan combine the remaining 2 cups of Merlot with the shallots and beach plum jam or currant jelly and boil until reduced by half. Add the chicken broth and the reserved plum flesh. Bring the mixture to a boil again and season with salt and pepper. Strain mixture into a small dish and hold for service.

4. Remove the duck legs from the marinade and pat dry. Place them on a baking pan and brush with honey. Sprinkle the legs with coarse salt and pepper and roast at 400°F for 1 hour. They will throw off a fair amount of fat and become very dark. Remove the duck legs from the oven and place on a clean sheet pan to cool.

5. When the duck legs are cool enough to handle, make a cut on the underside with a sharp knife, following the leg and thigh bone. Twist out the bones with your fingers, being careful not to tear the skin. Reheat the boned duck and serve the sauce on the side.

Serves 6. Pair with a Long Island Merlot.

SMALL PRODUCERS OF THE NORTH FORK

vinified at Raphael's winery by veteran Long Island winemaker Richard Olsen-Harbich.

Croteaux Vineyards' first three releases, made from the 2006 vintage, were Merlot 3 Rosé, Merlot 181 Rosé, and Merlot 314 Rosé. The numbers represent which Merlot clone produced the fruit that went into the wine. All three wines have received very favorable reviews.

Croteaux Vineyards
1450 South Harbor Road, Southold
(631) 765-6099
www.croteaux.com
Open year-round
Owners: Michael and Paula Croteau
Winemaker: Richard Olsen-Harbich
Founded: 2003
Acres planted: 10½
Varieties grown: Sauvignon Blanc, Cabernet Franc, Merlot
Long Island Wine Council member

CROTEAUX VINEYARDS

"Rosé on Purpose," Croteaux Vineyards' motto, perfectly expresses the philosophy that motivates proprietors Michael and Paula Croteau. Their vineyards were planted with the singular aim of producing enjoyable rosé wines that are crisp, dry, and fruity.

Michael, a graphic artist who has designed labels and packaging for many of the region's wineries, carefully chose particular clones of Merlot, Cabernet Franc, and Sauvignon Blanc vines. More than ten acres of the fourteen-acre vineyard, located on two historic Southold farms, were planted in 2003. The fruit is hand-harvested at optimum ripeness and

JASON'S VINEYARD

The Jason in Jason's Vineyard is Jason Damianos, a second-generation Long Island vineyard owner who grew up working at Pindar, his family's Peconic vineyard and winery. In 1996, after an extensive and distinguished education in viticulture and winemaking in California and France, he returned to the North Fork and established his own vineyard while supervising wine production at Pindar and his family's other winery, Duck Walk.

Jason says his vineyard was the first on Long Island to be planted with the tighter spacing he saw during his studies in France, which master viticulturists there say results in fewer and riper grape clusters. Only the best French clones were planted on twenty acres on the Main Road in Jamesport.

Jason's Vineyard currently produces Merlot, Chardonnay, Cabernet Sauvignon, and a Meritage Bordeaux blend. As this is written, Cabernet Sauvignon Port is about to be released. All of the wines in current release have won awards and high ratings. Most recently, the Beverage Tasting Institute gave the 2001 Cabernet Sauvignon 88 points and the 2000 Meritage 89 points; silver medals were awarded to the same two wines by Tasters Guild International; and the 2000 Chardonnay won a gold medal in Jerry Mead's New World International competition.

A tasting room and wine-production facility are slated to open by spring 2009. Jason's Vineyard wines are available at Pindar, Duck Walk, Duck Walk North, and area wine stores and through the Web site.

Jason's Vineyard
Main Road, Jamesport
(631) 926-8486
www.jasonsvineyard.com
Owner/winemaker: Jason Damianos
Founded: 1997
Acres planted: 20
Varieties grown: Chardonnay, Cabernet Franc, Cabernet Sauvignon, Malbec, Merlot
Long Island Wine Council member

SCAROLA VINEYARDS

The Scarola family's winemaking heritage goes back to a small family farm, or *masseria*, on Italy's Adriatic coast. Frank Scarola, who operates Scarola Vineyards with his wife, Donna, and other family members, grew up in Queens, surrounded by aunts, uncles, and cousins. The whole family worked the fertile land in their backyard, growing fruits and vegetables, raising chickens and ducks, and making wine.

Throughout his still-active career as a software designer, Frank says he has longed to reclaim his connection to the land. So in 2003, when he met master Long Island winemaker Roman Roth, Frank asked if Roman would be his consultant, and Scarola Vineyards was born.

Using top-quality fruit purchased from local growers, Scarola Vineyards has so far produced Chardonnay, Merlot, and Cabernet Franc. Each of these wines has won award medals in international competitions. In 2007 two vintages of Masseria Merlot won silver, two vintages of Cappella Chardonnay earned silver and bronze, and Cabernet Franc won bronze.

The Scarolas are planting their own six-acre vineyard in Southold and plan to open a tasting room. Currently only five hundred cases are produced each year; most is sold to restaurants and directly to customers.

Scarola Vineyards
Main Road, Southold
(631) 335-4199
frank@scarolavineyards.com
www.scarolavineyards.com
Owner: Frank Scarola
Winemaker: Roman Roth
Founded: 2003
Acres planted: 6
Grapes purchased from various Long Island vineyards
Long Island Wine Council member

DUCK WALK VINEYARDS

EAST OF SOUTHAMPTON, NEAR THE SMALL VILLAGE OF WATER MILL, STANDS A RAMBLING, NORMAN-STYLE, REDBRICK CHÂTEAU WITH tall, narrow windows, a copper roof oxidized to dusty aqua, and double glass doors surmounted by a windowed arch and flanked by towering evergreens. Built in 1986 by its first owner, this grand winery was bought by Dr. Herodotus "Dan" Damianos, owner of Pindar Vineyards on the North Fork, and reopened as Duck Walk Vineyards in 1994 under the management of his eldest son, Alexander.

The Old World theme continues into the cavernous tasting room, where a soaring, wood-paneled ceiling presides over wooden floors, a long wooden tasting bar, pale walls hung with traditional sconces and colorful art deco and art nouveau prints, and ranks of wine bottles on wooden tables.

Out back, a veranda overlooking the vineyard

provides an inviting place to sit with a glass of wine and enjoy live music on summer weekends.

Co-owner and General Manager, Alexander Damianos

In early May, as tender leaf buds were just beginning to emerge from the vines, Alex Damianos sat with a visitor in his office at Duck Walk North to talk about growing up in the Long Island wine business.

The idea of making wine had been in the back of his father's mind for a long time, Alex says. "It always intrigued my father, because he studied in Europe, at the University of Bologna in Italy. He had to learn Italian before he could understand classes for medical school, and in Italy he became fond of wines from the different regions."

"When he bought our first house—in 1966–67, in Stony Brook—there was a grape arbor on the property, and every other year, without doing any sprays or anything, you'd get these incredible clusters of grapes." Seeing how well grapes grew on Long Island, Alex says, inspired his father to pursue his dream.

"I was about eleven years old when he purchased his first forty acres of farmland, a former potato farm," Alex recalls. "That's where the Pindar winery and tasting room are today. That property stretched from the Main Road to Sound Avenue, or Route 48. My dad brought me out to show me the land where he was eventually going to plant a vineyard."

Alex smiles broadly as he relates what happened that day: "Dad had an old, white Mercedes. We're

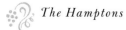

on Sound Avenue, and there's a dirt road that stretches from Sound Avenue to where the barns and everything are, which were converted into the tasting room. It had rained the day before, and I convinced my dad to take the road. I said, 'Dad, we can get through, we can get through!'

"As soon as we got on the road, we sank right down. At the time out here, he was, like, 'the doctor from the city,' and he had on a three-piece suit, and he gets out and is up to his knees in mud! We're trying to pull the car out. We couldn't, so we both got onto Sound Avenue and started walking west and finally came to a farm. There was an old potato farmer fixing his tractor, and we explained to him what had happened, and he said, 'Get on the back.' So both of us—he's in his three-piece suit, mud on our hands—we climb on the back of the tractor and we get there and he pulls us out.

"Dad wasn't happy with me, although he did make the decision to go down this road!" Alex says with a laugh, and then he continues describing the early years.

"We planted our first five acres right to the side of where the tasting room at Pindar is. At the time, we had a consultant take care of the five acres, and after about a year my dad said it would be less expensive for us to get our own crew—because the next year we were planning on planting thirty acres—to take care of it. So we bought the tractors, we bought everything needed to take care of a vineyard.

"But that first five acres, I remember my dad used to bring my brother, myself, and my mom out every Saturday and Sunday, and we'd be weeding this five acres with hoes, or by hand—it was crazy!

"I probably worked just about every weekend and every summer, except for when I went away to college, in the vineyards. From usually about six thirty, seven in the morning to sometimes eight, nine o'clock at night, because things had to get done.

"I did every part of the business," Alex recounts. "I tied vines, I pounded posts, I nailed in staples to put up wires, I rototilled. I did everything. It wasn't, like, an hour. I didn't work for an hour and get bored; I was out there with the workers." During his high school years, Alex invited friends from the Stony Brook School to make extra money by joining him on the weekends.

Alex went to the University of Bridgeport in Connecticut, where he earned a bachelor of science in management and marketing. Then he took over the management of the Pindar wine store in Port Jefferson and doubled sales the first year. While working up to fifty hours a week at the store, he obtained dual MBAs in general business studies and total quality management at Dowling College.

"There was not really room for me at Pindar with the sort of credentials that I had," Alex recalls. "There wasn't going to be a position created just because I'm the doctor's son; he doesn't do that. However, at the same time, my dad had made several offers for a building that was an operational winery, but it was under bankruptcy. Barclays Bank was running it. It was in Water Mill. It was called, at the time, Southampton Winery."

Eventually the bank accepted Dr. Dan's offer. When he asked Alex if he wanted to manage the new business, Alex was ready.

"In fourteen years," he says with evident pride, "I made Duck Walk a well-known name on Long Island. And that's through very hard work. I would

do tours—when somebody would walk in the door and ask, 'Can I have a tour?' I would give a tour. Finally, I was killing myself, and my dad was like, 'Do scheduled tours. Make it twelve, two, four . . .' So I did that. I've given over a thousand tours, and my tours are pretty good. It expresses what we've done to make Duck Walk successful.

"In about eight years," he goes on, "we grew from one of the smallest vineyards—because we had to replant most of the vineyards—to the second-largest vineyard on Long Island. We have 150

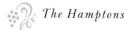

acres. We grow close to fourteen different varieties of grapes. Everything that we produce and grow on Long Island is made into wine that you taste in our tasting room. None of the grapes are purchased from other vineyards, including Pindar, and we're proud of that."

The Wines

Duck Walk wines are made by John Friszolowski and Dan Pantaleo under the supervision of Alex's brother Jason Damianos, director of winemaking for both Duck Walk and Pindar. A wide range of styles is offered, from varietals to Bordeaux- and Burgundy-style blends, semisweet table wines, and lush dessert wines.

All three white varietals currently on the wine list have won medals. The 2005 Chardonnay earned silver and bronze, as well as a "Best Buy" recommendation, from the *New York Times*. The 2006 Pinot Grigio has won gold and silver; the 2005 Sauvignon Blanc, silver and bronze. In white blends Duck Walk offers the dry Southampton White and off-dry Windmill White.

Falling between white and red is a fruity rosé called Windmill Blush.

Red varietals include 2005 Pinot Meunier and Gatsby Red, a semisweet, nonvintage table wine. The 2004 Merlot has won gold, silver, and bronze medals, and the limited-production 2004 Reserve Merlot boasts a gold and two silvers. In Cabernet Sauvignon both the 2005 and the 2004 limited-production bottlings earned gold. Also produced in limited amounts were 2005 Pinot Noir and a 2003 Meritage Bordeaux blend, newly released as of this writing. Another dry blend, Windmill Red, won a gold medal.

Duck Walk is well known for its dessert wines; all four currently on the list have brought home at least one medal. Perhaps the most unusual of these wines is Blueberry Port; its 2006 vintage won gold and bronze medals. Gold also went to Boysenberry Dessert Wine and 2005 Aphrodite, which picked up a silver as well. The 2005 vintage of Aphrodite is sold out, but the 2007 is available.

Duck Walk Vineyards
Montauk Highway, Water Mill
(631) 726-7555
info@duckwalk.com
www.duckwalk.com
Open year-round
Owner: Dr. Herodotus Damianos and family
Winemakers: John Friszolowski and Dan Pantaleo
Director of winemaking: Jason Damianos
Founded: 1994
Acres planted: 150
Varieties grown: Chardonnay, Pinot Grigio, Gewürztraminer, Sauvignon Blanc, Semillon, Cabernet Sauvignon, Malbec, Merlot, Pinot Meunier, Pinot Noir
Long Island Wine Council member

Seared Diver Sea Scallops with Sweet-Corn Polenta, Sea Bean–Shiitake Ragout, and Basil Oil

The Plaza Café, Southampton | *Doug Gulija, chef*

Basil Oil

>   3 cups lightly packed fresh basil leaves, plus more for garnish
>   2 cups grape seed oil

Sweet-Corn Polenta

>   2½ cups polenta
>   8 ounces butter, cubed
>   12–15 ears of fresh corn, grated
>   Brown sugar to taste
>   Salt and pepper

Scallops

>   20 U-10* diver sea scallops, cleaned
>   Salt and pepper
>   1 pound sea beans (Salicornia)
>   5 pounds fresh shiitake mushrooms, destemmed, roasted, and sliced
>   White wine, for deglazing

>   *Under 10 scallops per pound

1. Blanch and shock basil; puree in blender with oil. Let stand overnight and then strain.
2. Bring 2 quarts water and polenta to simmer and cook until thickened. Add butter; fold in grated corn and juices. Adjust seasoning with brown sugar, salt, and pepper.
3. Season scallops with salt and pepper and sear in a hot pan until golden on one side. Turn scallops and add sea beans and shiitakes, sautéing for about 1 minute; deglaze with white wine.
4. Portion polenta the in center of each bowl and top with a scallop. Top each scallop with the vegetable mixture and pan juices; surround with basil oil and garnish with fresh basil.

Serves 20. Pair with a Long Island Sauvignon Blanc or stainless steel–fermented Chardonnay.

The annual Hamptons Wine & Food Festival cook-off highlights local wine and produce.

CHANNING DAUGHTERS WINERY

A T CHANNING DAUGHTERS ART AND WINE MEET IN AN ORIGINAL WAY: THE GROUNDS ARE ADORNED WITH ASTONISHING SCULPTURES. A tree trunk carved into a two-headed dragon towers into the sky. Bas-relief children climb another trunk, their carved hands pulling down a curtain decorated with grape clusters. An impossibly tall human figure stands on tree-branch legs near a giant spear of asparagus.

These are the works of Walter Channing, Harvard-educated venture capitalist, sculptor of salvaged wood, and founder of the vineyard and winery named for his four daughters: Francesca, Isabella, Sylvia, and Nina. In the years since he planted his first vines in 1982, Walter has taken on three partners who run Channing Daughters while he continues his career and his avocation: turning salvaged wood into sculptures that have been shown in prestigious galleries in the United States and abroad since 1975.

Partners Larry Perrine, Christopher Tracy, and Allison Dubin

On a perfect spring day, with birds twittering in the background, a visitor sat with Walter Channing's three partners on the shady brick patio in front of the tasting room for a wide-ranging conversation about their personal journeys in the world of wine, what led them to Channing Daughters, and what excites them about their work at the winery.

They don't like to use titles here, but officially Larry Perrine is the CEO, Allison Dubin is the general manager, and Christopher Tracy is the winemaker.

"It should start with Larry," Christopher declares. "If it weren't for Larry, not only wouldn't the winery exist, but we wouldn't be here as well, because he brought us in."

"He's been so generous with his knowledge and his spirit," says Allison, "with everything from training people in the vineyards to working with Cornell, to working on the Wine and Grape Foundation, to working with the governor."

When it's Larry's turn, he opens with self-deprecating humor. "That's what comes with age," he says. Then, prompted to outline the path that led him to Long Island, he begins, "As a young person I was interested in wine, in my early twenties, growing up in California. I took a lot of my initial interest and inspiration from the brand-new little wineries in northern California."

He studied agriculture and worked in that field, but around age thirty he decided to return to his first love, wine. Instead of going back to California, Larry was drawn to the Finger Lakes by an article in the *New York Times* about a few winemakers there. "They were setting out new quality standards, growing *vinifera* grapes in New York, and there was a revolution going on. I was still young and

enthusiastic, and I thought, 'Why not go there and do that rather than go home to the more established districts? Have an adventure.' I've had about twenty-seven years of adventure now."

After completing his graduate work at Cornell University in the early 1980s, Larry moved to the North Fork, where he worked for the Mudd family, who had been planting vineyards since 1974. After doing viticultural research at Cornell's Riverhead farm laboratory and helping to found a North Fork vineyard, he began doing more consulting. That was when a mutual friend introduced him to Walter Channing.

"Walter had a little vineyard he was more or less in over his head on," Larry says. He was struggling a little bit, and I was a person who could take over at that point and get it up to snuff." Eventually the two became partners in the new enterprise.

"We did fairly well for about five years on that path," Larry continues, "and then Christopher and Allison came into our lives. After a short courtship we realized that this was something we really wanted to do together, and that was the pivotal moment that galvanized the transformation of the business from a dream that was partially realized into one that's fully realized. And now Channing Daughters has a very, very talented staff and group of owners, because we're all owners in the company that I really believe is setting the pace for innovation in the industry and pushing the envelope of what kinds of wines can be made here."

Christopher and Allison grew up on opposite coasts, Christopher in the San Francisco Bay area, Allison in New York City and eastern Long Island; but both were exposed to good food and wine at home and abroad. Christopher's parents owned a vineyard in Napa, and he and his mom made their own wine in garbage cans. His path converged with Allison's in graduate theater school in New York City, where they wrote restaurant reviews so they could eat and drink in good restaurants. Christopher decided to go to cooking school and graduated from the French Culinary Institute at the top of his class.

"Allison and I were collecting wine and buying wine and studying wine and bemoaning the fact that we were far away from a wine region when we really weren't," Christopher says.

The couple begin visiting every winery on the East End. "We walked in here one day," recalls Christopher, "and Larry had some rubber boots on and was cleaning some stuff up in the back, and we struck up a conversation, and . . ."

Allison leaps in: ". . . two hours later we were members of the wine club, we were coming back next week, and we had tried all these various wines."

"We joined the wine club," Christopher goes on, "and within six months or so there was a potential for about ten to fifteen people to join something we used to do called Team Merlot, where those people would come out once a month and be part of the whole process, from coming out in February and pruning, to coming out and removing leaves after fruit set, to blending the wine, bottling the wine, whatever it was. And as that happened we got to be friends with Larry, and . . ."

Christopher Tracy (left), Allison Dubin, and Larry Perrine

Allison: "...we always stayed later than everyone else and talked his ear off for hours ..."

Christopher: ". . . and started eating and drinking, and then we started asking questions about why they were doing certain things and not other things. I was curious about doing an indigenous-yeast Chardonnay, and Larry said, 'Well, you want to do it?' And I said, 'Yeah!' So we created our first L'Enfant Sauvage in 2001, even though we weren't working here at the time. I was able to make four barrels of that wine, and one thing led to another, and those projects had some success.

"Then September 11 happened...and the next thing we knew, there was an opportunity to come out here. Larry hired us and we moved out in March of

'02 full-time. I finished the '01 wines, and I've been making the vintages since."

The three give Walter a good deal of credit for the sense of experimentation that prevails here. "One of the things about Walter—he's the fourth partner, the majority partner," Christopher begins, "he's a very creative guy and very astute. I think one of his great talents, too, is to know when to step back, and he gave Larry very much a blank slate to create the initial ideas of the white wines and planting new varieties.

"I felt that that was extended to us when we came on—to create new wines, new products, to talk about new possibilities in the vineyard. That kind of creative, synergistic work is what I think makes

Channing Daughters Winery special," Christopher concludes.

"No one has a precise job description," Larry says. "We gave up that kind of stuff years ago when we realized we didn't need to work that way. It's not a large company, not a corporate structure."

"It's more dynamic than that," Christopher adds. "And that transfers into the work in the vineyard and in the cellar, too, because we can turn in any direction, whether it's on the crush pad at fruit reception, and we decide that this needs to go to a different place than we thought, or maybe even make something entirely new. We think like that, on our feet, creatively. We aren't afraid to take some chances, to push the envelope, and even occasionally to make some mistakes."

Larry adds, "Periodically we'll get into a conversation about wine, and we'll say, 'What if?' And, like Christopher said, occasionally that occurs right on the reception pad during harvest: 'What if we did this?' And some of the answers became new wines we had only imagined in the moment, certainly based on ideas that we had from some other place and some other time.

"But it's not a static situation; it's an evolving world we live in, and that's kind of fun. We're not highly structured and hidebound, as some traditional districts are. They're making great wines, but in some of the more traditional districts like Burgundy, there are basically a couple of wines made there from just a couple of grape varieties, and there really aren't too many variants on it at all. That's to be celebrated for its historical high quality, but we live in a different world where we can do whatever we choose, and that's what makes it really, really satisfying and exciting."

The Wines

Channing Daughters produces wine from grapes grown on its own estate and the estate vineyards of North Fork growing partners Steve and Dave Mudd. The Bridgehampton vines are meticulously tended by vineyard manager Abel Lopez. That same care is evident in the winery, where traditional, artisanal winemaking methods are used, from gently pressing whole clusters of white grapes to stomping red grapes by foot.

The experimentation celebrated at Channing Daughters also applies in the vineyard, where some blocks contain several different grape varieties growing together, a practice known as complanting, and others are planted with different clones of the same variety, each chosen for its particular characteristics.

The winery produces about seven thousand cases annually of more than twenty wines. Their unusual whites, especially the unique blends, draw high praise from wine critics.

Whites made in most vintages include Mudd Vineyard Sauvignon Blanc, Pinot Grigio, Tocai Friulano, Sauvignon, steel-fermented Scuttlehole Chardonnay, L'Enfant Sauvage Chardonnay, barrel-fermented Brick Kiln Chardonnay, and seven blends:

Sylvanus, Vino Bianco, Mosaica, Cuvée Tropical, Clones, Envelope, and Meditazione.

A trio of rosés, known collectively as Tre Rosati, comprises Rosato di Cabernet Franc, Rosato di Merlot, and Rosato di Cabernet Sauvignon.

Reds usually on the wine list include blends Rosso Fresco, Sculpture Garden, Research Cab, MUDD, and Over & Over–Variation 1. Blaufrankisch rounds out the offerings.

Channing Daughters Winery
1927 Scuttlehole Road, Bridgehampton
(631) 537-7224
info@channingdaughters.com
www.channingdaughters.com
Open year-round; appointments required for groups larger than six
Owners: Walter Channing, Larry Perrine, Allison Dubin, and Christopher Tracy
Winemaker: Christopher Tracy
Founded: 1997
Acres planted: 25
Major varieties grown: Chardonnay, Gewürztraminer, Pinot Bianco, Pinot Grigio, Sauvignon Blanc, Semillon, Tocai Friulano, Viognier, Blaufrankisch, Cabernet Franc, Cabernet Sauvignon, Merlot, Pinot Noir, Syrah
Long Island Wine Council member

WÖLFFER ESTATE VINEYARD

Not far off Montauk Highway, on the road leading from Sagaponack to Sag Harbor, a Tuscan-style winery with ochre walls and Mediterranean-blue shutters sits on a hill, presiding with Old World grace over fifty acres of meticulously tended vines. Stone steps lead up a landscaped slope, past a fountain and two massive stone urns planted with stately evergreens, to a heavy wooden door with a wrought-iron pull. Inside, your eyes are drawn to the view through French doors to a covered flagstone patio overlooking the vineyard.

Wölffer's tasting room, while grand and elegant, feels intimate and welcoming at the same time. A simple wooden table serves as a tasting bar. There are square stools to perch on, but other seating areas beckon: ladder-backed chairs at a round table, a comfy sofa facing two overstuffed chairs, and that irresistible patio. Overhead, century-old wooden beams and ironwork chandeliers add to the Old World ambience.

A German-born entrepreneurial venture capitalist with a worldwide business background, Christian Wölffer, planted his first sixteen acres of grapes in 1988 with no intention of founding a world-class winery; he planned to sell his grapes to others. But like many other Long Island winery owners, he was willingly seduced by the allure of the vineyard and a dream of making wonderful wine in one of the most beautiful settings on Earth.

The Winemaker, Roman Roth

In Roman Roth, who is also from Germany, Christian found a winemaker whose vision matched his own: Create the finest possible wines, combining the traditions of the Old World with the unique qualities of the grapes grown in their vineyard. On a blustery day in early April, following a private tasting in the wine library, Roman and a visitor settled at a semicircular tasting table set in a niche in the wall of the vaulted barrel cellar. Over lunch and a glass of superb Wölffer Merlot, they talked about his background and his career at Wölffer Estate.

Roman began studying winemaking in Germany in 1982, as a sixteen-year-old apprentice. "It really gave me the foundation of being detail oriented, of multitasking," he says, "because it was a very quality-oriented winery, but of fairly big size, too, so that every drop and every

bottle and every barrel—I mean, you really were after every detail."

In 1986 he left Germany for California's Napa Valley. "I wasn't too impressed with the New World," he says, "how anything goes and how certain things—no rules apply. You can grow anything you want; if you want to make something, you can go for it. So that was interesting.

"And then, what was even more important, I think, was a trip to Australia, where I worked at Rosemount Estate. The philosophy of winemaking was such an important search there. In Germany, of course, your grandfather already made the best wine, so you're making the same things, while in Australia, in the New World, you try to find what is the character, why do you do something?

"And I think I translated all that," Roman continues, "and I went back to Germany, to

Heidelberg, and had a great position there, at a winery which was a big winery, too, but they had a very high-quality small section inside the winery, where I worked.

"The bottom line is, I think that's why I'm here on Long Island: to make something that is very balanced and unique. This," Roman says intently, holding up a glass of deep, dark Merlot, "is very special; you can only do this on Long Island. California is a different climate; it's tough to make these elegant, balanced wines. Here, because we're on the same latitude as Madrid and Naples, we can get fabulous concentration, yet great elegance. And when you combine the two, to me that's what makes the greatest vintage. It may be a Riesling from Germany, a Burgundy, a Bordeaux—it doesn't matter; it's that combination between intensity and

playfulness. And I think that's why I've been here since 1992," he concludes.

When his guest asks what brought him to Long Island in the first place, Roman replies, "Christian was looking for a winemaker, and he looked here and in California, and he looked in Germany. We met in Germany, and he said, 'Buy whatever you have to buy, and do whatever you want to do. Just make the best wine.' "

Even though, at the time, Roman was about to leave Germany for Australia, Christian's offer proved too enticing to resist. Roman and his wife, Australian-born Dushy, came to Long Island.

"Also, why I'm here is the combination that Christian Wölffer has put together, the freedom that he gives me, the energy that he puts in behind it, too, when something exciting happens, like the wine we

just tasted, or the Premier Cru, for example," Roman says. "It's important that you have a proprietor who gets excited about something special." The Premier Cru is the estate's very highly regarded premium Merlot.

Roman works closely with vineyard manager Richard Pisacano—owner of Roanoke Vineyards on the North Fork—to bring in fruit of the highest quality. Their teamwork, Roman says, is key to the consistent style and quality of Wölffer's wines. And he believes that being in the Hamptons and so close to Manhattan pushes Long Island wineries to produce better and better wines, because the best wines from all over the world are available here. "The bar is set higher, which means you have to perform better," he says. "As a result, you constantly improve, rather than being happily satisfied somewhere along the way . . . and that's an important thing.

"As the vineyard is getting older," he continues, "as you get more experience with these vineyards—I mean Richie and myself—we've gotten bolder and bolder and pushed more and more towards wines that are more intensified, more classic."

According to Roman, the soil at the top of their sloping vineyard site—a six- or seven-foot layer of clay, silt, and what is known as Bridgehampton loam—gives Wölffer's wines their finesse. "It is a great, unique spot," he says. "We always say, if you had to pick another vineyard anywhere in the Hamptons or Long Island, this would definitely be a spot we would pick. It sounds like a commercial; it sounds a bit corny, maybe, but it is the truth. It is a unique spot for quality wines."

"The greatest thing right now," Roman says a moment later, "is young people who want to learn, who are excited about a region close by, who

don't fly to France or to Italy or California to see a vineyard; they come here. That has been another huge boost to make individual wines. We don't need to make wines that are mass-produced, that serve whole America, that serve some big distributor. We can make wines that have a story, that have character, that have one note that speaks out, and you identify it with that vintage, or with the winemaker, or with the style of the house. I think that's another specialty that's more and more now in huge demand."

The Wines

Wölffer Estate's wines consistently earn the highest praise and outstanding ratings from wine critics, restaurateurs, and customers.

Wines are offered under several labels, in ascending quality and price: La Ferme Martin, Reserve, Estate Selection, and varietal labels. The Premier Cru designation is reserved for the premium Merlot, which wine critics have compared favorably with the best of France. Often more than one vintage of the same wine will be available.

In Merlot, in addition to Premier Cru, Wölffer currently produces La Ferme Martin, Reserve, and Estate Selection. Merliance, a special Merlot made

by the Long Island Merlot Alliance, of which Wölffer is a member, is also available. Cabernet Franc and Pinot Noir under varietal labels round out the list of reds.

Falling between reds and whites is Rosé Table Wine, which garnered superlative reviews upon its 2007 release.

On the white wine list at this writing are La Ferme Martin, Reserve, and Estate Selection Chardonnay and varietally labeled Pinot Gris. Specialty whites include Cuvée Sparkling Wine Brut, made by the traditional Champagne method, and Late Harvest Chardonnay, a dessert wine.

Collectors and connoisseurs may want to purchase wines from Wölffer's library, which goes all the way back to the fabled 1995 vintage. At this writing, two vintages of Premier Cru are available from the library.

Wölffer Estate Vineyard
139 Sagg Road, Sagaponack
(631) 537-5106
info@wolffer.com
www.wolffer.com
Open year-round
Owner: Christian Wölffer
Winemaker: Roman Roth
Founded: 1988
Acres planted: 50
Varieties grown: Chardonnay, Pinot Grigio,
Cabernet Franc, Merlot, Pinot Noir
Long Island Wine Council member

SMALL PRODUCER OF THE HAMPTONS

THE GRAPES OF ROTH

German-born Roman Roth, winemaker at Wölffer Estate, launched his own label in 2006 with the release of The Grapes of Roth 2001 Merlot. That wine was greeted with superlative reviews and an outstanding score of 91 in *Wine Advocate*. The 2002 Merlot achieved a score of 92, the highest rating given by *Wine Advocate* to any New York wine.

Roman called his venture The Grapes of Roth not only as a pun on his name, but because he lives in Sag Harbor, where *The Grapes of Wrath* author John Steinbeck once lived. He says creating his own label is the fulfillment of a dream that became stronger once he felt completely settled in his personal and professional life and was looking for something more.

"I think The Grapes of Roth was that missing thing for me, to produce something that doesn't go away, no matter what happens," Roman says. "I mean, that is my wine. There is a very personal connection to every bottle and every person who tastes it.

"And there was a realization that, yes, Long Island is a world-class region and can make wines that stand up to the best, anytime, if you do things right, if you work hard, if you select, if you go the extra mile. It gave me the confidence to say, yes, I do want to put my money, my future into this, because I felt it is something very special to bet on, to put both feet into it.

"Thanks to Christian Wölffer, who lets me do that. I think it's important, too, that he is very creative. He has, in many ways, taught me different things about life, and that has expressed itself in creating something unique for myself, too," Roman concludes.

As this is written, The Grapes of Roth is about to release its 2003 Merlot and has just released its first Riesling. Roman carefully chooses his fruit from select North Fork vineyards, has it harvested by hand, and meticulously handcrafts his wines in very limited quantities. They can be found at Roanoke Vineyards on the North Fork, but most is sold through a mailing list and the Web site.

The Grapes of Roth
(631) 725-7999
info@thegrapesofroth.com
www.thegrapesofroth.com
Owners: Roman and Dushy Roth
Founded: 2001
Long Island Wine Council member

FEATURED RESTAURANTS
AND CHEF

Long Island Wine Council
Steven Bate, Executive Director
P.O. Box 600
Riverhead, NY 11901
(631) 722-2220
info@liwines.com
www.liwines.com

Long Island Wine Press
Times/Review Newspapers
P.O. Box 1500
Mattituck, NY 11952
(631) 298-3200
mail@liwinepress.com
www.liwinepress.com

Stony Brook Center for Wine, Food, and Culture
Louisa Hargrave, Director
Contact: Ginny Clancy, Program Coordinator
Stony Brook University
(631) 632-9404
ginny.clancy@stonybrook.edu
www.sunysb.edu/sb/winecenter

Jedediah Hawkins Inn
400 South Jamesport Avenue
Jamesport, NY 11947
(631) 722-2900
info@jedediahhawkinsinn.com
www.jedediahhawkinsinn.com

The North Fork Table & Inn
57225 Main Road
Southold, NY 11971
(631) 765-0177
info@northforktableandinn.com
www.northforktableandinn.com

The Plaza Café
61 Hill Street
Southampton, NY 11968
(631) 283-9323
www.plazacafe.us

John Ross
johncross@optonline.net

Shinn Estate Farmhouse
2000 Oregon Road
Mattituck, NY 11952
(631) 804-0367
shinvin@optonline.net
www.shinnfarmhouse.com

ACKNOWLEDGMENTS

FIRST AND FOREMOST, I'M GRATEFUL TO THE LONG ISLAND WINE COUNCIL AND ITS MEMBER WINERIES FOR THEIR ENTHUSIASM AND COOPERATION THROUGHOUT THIS PROJECT. Special thanks to the council for allowing the use of its "Long Island Wine Country" trademark and its map.

Many thanks to my husband, David, for his patience and encouragement; Louisa Hargrave for her wonderful foreword and friendship; Judi Betts for her invaluable moral support; Ann Marie and Marco Borghese for graciously arranging that memorable wine dinner; and Clovis Point for the beautiful Riedel wine glasses.

My gratitude goes to the chefs who generously shared their recipes, some of which were adapted for home cooks: John Ross for Lobster Stew, Oysters Baked in Garlic and Pernod, and Boneless Marinated Duck Legs with Roasted Plum Sauce; Tom Schaudel and Michael Ross of Jedediah Hawkins Inn for Handmade Ricotta Gnocchi with North Fork Farm Stand Vegetable Basil Broth and Reggiano and Seared Duck Breast with Citrus Glaze; Claudia Fleming of the North Fork Table & Inn for Strawberry-Rhubarb Cobbler and Spring Onion, Potato, and Goat Cheese Tart; Doug Gulija of the Plaza Café for Seared Diver Sea Scallops with Sweet-Corn Polenta, Sea Bean–Shiitake Ragout, and Basil Oil; and David Page and Barbara Shinn of Shinn Estate Farmhouse for Grilled Three-Cheese Sandwiches with Sunny Side-Up Duck Eggs. These individuals and restaurants are not responsible for any inadvertent errors or omissions.

Finally, it's been a pleasure to work with photographer Bruce Curtis; our agent, Rita Rosenkranz; and everyone at the Globe Pequot Press.

172

ABOUT THE AUTHOR

J ANE TAYLOR STARWOOD IS THE EDITOR OF THE *LONG ISLAND WINE PRESS,* PUBLISHED BY TIMES/ REVIEW NEWSPAPERS IN AFFILIATION WITH THE Long Island Wine Council. The first issue under her charge was awarded first place in its division in the New York Press Association's Better Newspaper Contest.

Before being named editor, Starwood wrote numerous *Wine Press* features about the people of Long Island Wine Country and various aspects of the local wine industry. Also a playwright, she has seen her plays produced at the historic Vail-Leavitt Music Hall in Riverhead. She is currently at work on a novel.

Starwood lives in Southold, New York, with her husband, David Starwood, a talented sculptor and artist.

ABOUT THE PHOTOGRAPHER

B RUCE CURTIS HAS CHRONICLED MANY OF THE SIGNIFICANT EVENTS OF RECENT DECADES. AS A PHOTOGRAPHER FOR *TIME* AND *LIFE,* HE has been on the front lines of a number of conflicts around the world. Some of his photographs are included in the Smithsonian Institution's permanent collection.

Also known for his work for *Sports Illustrated,* Curtis has received twenty-five awards for his photography. He has also been the exclusive photographer for more than forty books. One recent project is a large-format coffee-table book produced with the National Baseball Hall of Fame.